THE AGENT

The Truth Behind the Anti-Muslim Campaign in America

Dr. Ahmed Yousef
Caroline F. Keeble

UASR Publishing Group, Inc.
Springfield, VA; USA

Copyright 1999, United Association for Studies and Research
ISBN 1-882669-18-5

Published by:

United Association for Studies and Research (UASR)
P. O. Box 1210, Springfield, Va. 22003-1210
Tel: (703) 750-9011 Fax: (703) 750-9010
E-mail: uasr@aol.com
www.uasr.org

ACKNOWLEDGMENT

The authors thank and acknowledge all of their friends and colleagues for their contributions and support of this project. May God accept our efforts and reward us all with peace.

"With the Name of God, Who is both Gracious and Merciful

*I*n memory of Baby Salaam, who died the day of the Oklahoma bombing only hours after Steven Emerson stated on CBS news that the bombing was the work of "Islamic terrorists" and that Oklahoma was a center for Islamic terrorism. Baby Salaam's home was attacked by an angry mob seeking revenge against Arabs and Muslims. The terror that Baby Salaam's mother experienced caused her to go into premature labor, giving birth to Salaam two months prior to his fetal maturation date. When the Oklahoma bombing victims were memorialized, no one mentioned Baby Salaam even though he was also a casualty. May God receive his soul with joy, and may he meet God well pleased. Dedicated to the Arabs and Muslims of America who have sufferd with patience. Today, we breath.

TABLE OF CONTENTS

PART II

STEVEN EMERSON

PART III

CONCLUSION

*N*ever mind that most Islamic countries today are too poverty stricken, tyrannical and hopelessly inept militarily as well as scientifically to be much of a threat to anyone except their own citizens; and never mind that the most powerful of them are totally within the U.S. orbit. What matters to "experts" like Judith Miller, Samuel Huntington, Martin Kramer, Bernard Lewis, Daniel Pipes, Steven Emerson and Barry Rubin, plus a whole battery of Israeli academics, is to make sure that the "threat" is kept before our eyes, the better to excoriate Islam for terror, despotism and violence, while assuring themselves profitable consultancies, frequent TV appearances and book contracts. The Islamic threat is made to seem disproportionately fearsome, lending support to the thesis (which is an interesting parallel to anti-Semitic paranoia) that there is a worldwide conspiracy behind every explosion.

Prof. Edward W. Said, *A Devil Theory of Islam,* **The Nation,** August 1996

FOREWORD

By Richard H. Curtiss

Writer Steven Abram Emerson burst into American public consciousness by leveling alarming charges in a 1994 film, shown by many public television stations, entitled *Jihad in America*. The film made sensational allegations that a sinister network of foreign terrorists had insinuated itself into America's rapidly expanding Muslim community. Emerson charged that the various components of this network not only were raising funds for Palestinians resisting Israeli forces in the West Bank, Gaza and Southern Lebanon, but also were planning deadly acts of murder and sabotage within the United States itself.

For the very few Americans familiar with the embryonic national Islamic organizations and their leaders in the United States, and who could understand the Arabic words being spoken in the clips of speeches and songs at public meetings of those groups, the charges were ludicrous. Even the clips of more militant speeches before Islamic groups overseas were taken out of context. They dated back to the Soviet occupation of Afghanistan rather than any contemporary "holy war"

Richard Curtiss, a retired career U.S. foreign service officer, is executive editor of the *Washington Report on Middle East Affairs*, a monthly magazine published in Washington D.C.

1

against the West as implied by Emerson.

But the vast majority of Americans who knew few, if any, Muslims, and had never heard of any of these organizations, had little reason to disbelieve the inflammatory charges, particularly because they were made in a video carried without disclaimers by the normally reliable public television network.

Initially such charges by Emerson, a "terrorism expert" who seemingly had no first-hand familiarity with any Middle Eastern country or language except Israel and Hebrew, and a "journalist" who had never studied journalism, were given some credence by two major events that preceded the showing of his film. These were the World Trade Center bombing in which six Americans were killed on February 26, 1993, in New York City, and a conspiracy to bomb the United Nations building and FBI headquarters in Manhattan along with the Lincoln and Holland Tunnels, which was aborted by arrests of the plotters in New York and New Jersey in June, 1993.

The mysterious Middle Easterner, Ramzi Ahmad Yousef, who planned and directed the World Trade Center bombing and escaped to launch other largely unsuccessful terrorist initiatives in the Far East before he was captured in Pakistan and tried in the United States, seemed to conform with Emerson's warnings. And although other home-grown American "terrorism experts," some of whom, like Emerson, had Israeli connections, did not echo the most sensational of Emerson's charges regarding Muslims, they seemed to observe a kind of professional solidarity in not ridiculing Emerson's allegations either.

Ultimately, Emerson's hyper-active attempts to draw more media attention to himself brought about his professional undoing. Immediately after the Oklahoma City bombing in April, 1995, he implied on both CBS and CNN that it was the work of Muslims, even though the perpetrator, Tim McVeigh, a U.S. army veteran with neither Muslim nor Middle Eastern connections, was caught within days largely because a loose license plate on his getaway car caught a state trooper's attention.

Similarly, after Paris-bound TWA Flight 800 exploded off Long Island in July, 1996, Emerson said in media statements he was "confident" and had "no doubt whatsoever" that the plane was brought down by a bomb and suggested to Reuters that it could be the work of "the permanent floating (Islamic) military international." But after a painstaking investigation involving dredging up the aircraft, piece by piece, from the sea floor, the FBI and FAA ascribed the explosion not to a bomb or a missile but to an accidental electrical spark that ignited fumes in an empty fuel tank.

His own unprofessional deportment had largely discredited Emerson before this study was prepared. But this study reveals how Emerson achieved sufficient media credibility to have his astonishing and, as it turned out, poorly-documented film accepted by public television.

For example, both before and after he prepared the film many of Emerson's articles were printed in *The New Republic*, *The Atlantic Monthly* and, particularly, by the *U.S. News and World Report*, where he was employed from 1985 to 1989. All of these publications are owned by extremely pro-Israel real estate investor Mortimer Zuckerman. Zuckerman apparently used his real estate profits to purchase the publications. Very recently, Zuckerman added the *New York Daily News* to his media empire after previous efforts to purchase it were interrupted by the mysterious death of British media mogul Robert Maxwell, who had long-standing ties to the Mossad, Israel's CIA, according to Mossad defector Victor Ostrovsky. The death of Maxwell, who was having trouble putting together the newspaper's purchase price and who already apparently had looted his company's employee pension funds, resulted from a nighttime fall overboard a few hours after his personal yacht, on which he was the sole passenger, made a brief stop in the Canary Islands.

Emerson also served as a free-lance reporter for CNN and published articles in *The New York Times Magazine*, the *Arizona Republic*, the *San Diego Union-Tribune*, the *Wall Street Journal* (which still occasionally publishes his articles), and various Jewish publications. This study points out that in writing for mainstream publications Emerson is careful to be politically correct by acknowledging that the "terrorists" of whom he writes are deviating from the teachings of Islam, while he drops such disclaimers in writing for journals which share his alarmist views.

Emerson's articles all seem to imply that the "terrorists" he studies are motivated by a profound but generalized hatred of the West, and particularly of America. He does not acknowledge the much more widely held view that what unifies such activists is fury at the Israeli occupation of all of Palestine, and that their anger at the United States is a direct result of its virtually unconditional and unquestioning support for successive Israeli governments.

This study also documents the sources of funding not only for Emerson's efforts, but also for those of other anti-Islamic and pro-Israel media endeavors. Contrary to my own initial expectations, none of the publicly acknowledged funding sources seem directly connected to Israel, nor even to the so-called "neo-conservatives" who do have such connections and sympathies.

Such "neo-conservatives" initially identified themselves as "conservatives who voted for Franklin D. Roosevelt." My own observation is that, virtually without exception, those who identify themselves as "neo-conservatives" are nearly full-time apologists for Israel whose abandonment of liberal causes and views resulted solely from their insistence on maintaining sufficient U.S. military strength to intervene, when necessary, to defend Israel.

Instead some of the funding for Emerson comes from foundations publicly associated with the extreme U.S. right wing. Upon closer examination, however, it appears that some of the same foundations in the past funded studies that sought to document ties between secular Arab extremists and terrorists and the Soviet Union, raising legitimate questions as to whether their primary concerns were to alert Americans to threats to the United States from the Soviet Union, or to arouse American opposition to left-leaning Arab extremists who threatened Israel.

The Lynde and Harry Bradley Foundation, which provided $100,000 for Emerson's *Jihad in America* also has funded a study by Robert Satloff, Executive Director of the Washington Institute for Near East Affairs, a think tank spun off by directors of the American Israel Public Affairs Committee, Israel's principal Washington D.C. lobby. Further, this same foundation has also provided grants to the Foreign Policy Research Institute of Philadelphia, then headed by Daniel Pipes and an associate, Khaled Duran, who also was Emerson's collaborator in producing *Jihad in America*.

Whether the grants from such foundations to apologists for Israel or Muslim-bashers like Pipes, Emerson, and Duran come from overt sympathizers with Israel among the foundation officers or directors (as seems to be the case with the Bradley Foundation) or from "anxious for Armageddon" Christian fundamentalists (sharing the beliefs of Jerry Falwell or Pat Roberts), or both, cannot be documented with certainty. What this study does document, however, are names of these foundations and of some of the other books, films, and studies they have funded.

Other such foundations besides the Bradley Foundation include the Olin Foundation, which gave Emerson $20,000 in 1993 for a proposed book on *Mohammad's Army: the Rise of Islamic Fundamentalism*, Richard Mellon Scaife whose Carthage Foundation helped fund Emerson's Islamic Jihad film, and the Smith Richardson Foundation.

5

This study points out that all of these foundations also support Frank Gaffney's Center for Security Policy. Since Gaffney's organization consistently attacked and sought to undermine peace efforts between Israel's Labor government and Yasser Arafat's Palestinian Authority, this indicates that at least some persons making the grants for all of these groups understand clearly that their funds are being used to support extreme right wing causes and undermine land-for-peace proponents in Israel.

Lest there be any doubt where Gaffney is coming from, as this study points out, his board of directors includes former AIPAC director Morris J. Amitay. Gaffney's Center for Security Policy also receives funding from the Irving I. Moskowitz foundation. Moskowitz has funded real estate takeovers in East Jerusalem by Israeli extremists such as Ariel Sharon and is funding Jewish settlement in East Jerusalem's Ras Al Amoud neighborhood where Palestinians are being evicted and their residences are being demolished.

Moskowitz also funded and was present for the 1997 opening of the tunnel along the foundations of the Haram Al Sharif, the third most holy place in Islam, which set off extremely bloody fighting between Israeli troops and protesting Palestinians and eventually also involved armed intervention against the Israeli forces by Palestinian Authority police. If the above named foundations all have Gaffney's organization in common, some of the other organizations which benefit from their grants also are eye openers. According to the study, Richard Mellon Scaife bankrolls the Sarah Scaife Foundation, the Carthage Foundation, and the Align Foundation which, in turn, provide grants for the Heritage Foundation, the Cato Institute, the Center for Strategic and International Studies (CSIS), the American Spectator, and Accuracy in Media (AIM).

Together with the Scaife foundations, the Smith Richardson Foundation and the Bradley and Olin Foundations are, according to this study, often called the "four sisters of conservative philanthropy." This study also names the Adolph Coors Foundation, which supports conservative think tanks, and the Koch Family Foundation as following "similar funding patterns for conservative and libertarian causes."

Other pro-Israel or anti-Muslim American and anti-Arab American efforts funded by these foundations provide further disturbing evidence that some of their efforts have little to do with conservative American causes, and much to do with Israeli extremism.

For example, the Bradley Foundation funded Steven Kaplan's widely-publicized book, *The Arabists: The Romance of an American Elite*, whose message seemed to be to dismiss critics within the State Department of the long-standing pro-Israel tilt in U.S. foreign policy as at best eccentrics and at worst anti-semites. Kaplan received Olin and Smith Richardson foundation funding for other book projects.

The study reports that The Program on National Security Affairs of Dr. Samuel Huntingdon, originator of much-discussed predictions of a bloody "Clash of Civilizations" between Islam and the West, received $200,000 from the Bradley Foundation in 1990 and, allegedly, $2.5 million in Olin funds.

Similarly, the pro-Israel and anti-Arab Foreign Policy Research Institute in Philadelphia received between 1990 and 1994, while it was directed by Pipes, an annual grant of $75,000 from Scaife, half a million dollars from Bradley, $60,000 from Olin and nearly $300,000 from Smith Richardson.

In the same vein, the Institute for International Studies in Washington D.C., which publishes Khalid Duran's journal, *TransState Islam*, received in 1993 and 1994 $235,000 from the Bradley, Olin and Smith Richardson Foundations.

Just as this study documents the similar funding patterns for pro-Israel projects by the major foundations named above, and the maze of subsidiary foundations they support, it names other journalists and scholars who allegedly have assisted with pro-Israel projects initiated by Emerson, Pipes, and Duran. Among these are prominent Orientalist scholar Bernard Lewis (whose son, Michael, has been the long-time head of AIPAC's opposition research department), Patrick Clawson, who formerly was associated with Pipes' Foreign Policy Research Institute and now is on the faculty of the U.S. government's National Defense University, nationally syndicated columnist Charles Krauthammer, and Barry Rubin, an American writer now living in Israel.

It could be argued that just as Emerson's 14 minutes of media fame seem to have passed, other propagandists named in this study may also lose their mainstream media access as their motives are exposed. Similarly, the foundations funding them may lose their credibility as the bias in their donation patterns is revealed. Unfortunately, however, the general public rarely is aware of the source of funding for such "experts" and their studies, and new names and faces undoubtedly will appear to partake of the same tainted grants.

Meanwhile, in addition to being the witting or unwitting catalysts for hundreds of attacks on innocent Muslim Americans and their property in many parts of the United States, Emerson and his ilk already have done lasting damage to the credibility of the United States and its legal system.

For example, arrests by Israeli authorities on trumped-up charges of American citizens of Palestinian extraction who are visiting their families in the Holy Land are becoming increasingly frequent. In most cases these Arab Americans are subjected to torture until they "confess" to whatever crimes they allegedly have committed. Israel is the only country in the world where the use of torture—which it calls "mild physical coercion"—to obtain confessions not only is practiced but actually is codified in Israeli law.

Some of these American citizens presently are serving long prison sentences on the basis of such coerced confessions. While

U.S. consular officials in Tel Aviv and Jerusalem eventually obtain access to detained Americans, the Emerson accusations may have contributed to an almost unconscious atmosphere of "where there's smoke there's fire" that may reduce the zeal of such American officials to protect the rights of U.S. citizens.

Even more corrosive of constitutional rights enjoyed by all American citizens is the anti-terrorism and effective death penalty act. This law was passed by Congress and signed by President Bill Clinton in 1996 in the wake of terrorist bombings and after videotapes of *Jihad in America* had been circulated to all 435 members of the House of Representatives at Carthage Foundation expense. It permits the use of secret evidence in deportation hearings against resident aliens in the United States who have not yet obtained U.S. citizenship.

Several legal residents of the U.S. have languished for as long as three years in prison in various parts of the United States on charges which neither they nor their lawyers are allowed to see, and which are leveled by persons whose identity neither they nor their lawyers are allowed to learn. Such a law, which undoubtedly will be repealed or amended at some future time when sanity prevails, could have been passed only under the conditions of near hysteria that prevailed after the bombings of the 90s, further whipped up by Emerson's charges.

Since few Americans are aware of the violations of constitutional rights being suffered by resident aliens in the United States, this study fills an urgent need. It exposes how and at whose behest such abridgments of U.S. freedom have come about.

Another result of the activities of people like Steven Emerson is the Freedom from Religious Persecution Act. Its primary instigator is Michael Horowitz who, like Emerson, is Jewish, although the act's ostensible purpose is to enact sanctions against countries where Christian minorities suffer discrimination. The Act has been criticized by the National

Council of Churches, the U.S. State Department, and representatives of such Christian minorities in non-Christian countries as the Copts of Egypt.

Nevertheless, the act was passed by the U.S. House of Representatives on May 14, 1998. It professes concern about Christians in China and Muslim countries but, revealingly, makes no mention whatsoever of Israeli persecution of the Christians of Palestine, whose leaders would welcome and have specifically solicited such U.S. concern.

Interestingly, in the *Atlantic Monthly* Horowitz is quoted as paying tribute to, in his words, a "handful of people" who, he says, began "the whole transformation of Conservative philosophy." Those he names are Richard Larry, grant director for the Sarah Scaife Foundation; Michael Joyce, grant director for the Olin Foundation, and Leslie Lenkowsky, "who once controlled grant awards for the Smith Richardson Foundation." It is significant that he names no individual from the Bradley Foundation, whose primary purpose seems to be the funding of American projects in support of Israel.

Among American Muslims, many of whom are highly trained professionals, it has become almost a cliche to fault their U.S. brethren as a whole for lack of concern for their own civil rights and inattention to detail except in matters directly pertaining to individual educational and career advancement.

Whether or not such charges have been justified in the past, this study by a small Islamic think tank in the U.S. national capital area is an obvious, and welcome, exception to any such generalizations. It provides a detailed examination of one of the most persistent defamers of American Muslims, as individuals and as a community.

This expose includes a careful documentation of the media outlets that have made themselves available to Steven Emerson and his associates. Even more revealing, and valuable, is the listing of the foundations which support Steven

Emerson and the writers and scholars who share his agenda.

It is this writer's hope that some of the directors, trustees, and executives of these foundations will be as profoundly surprised and disturbed as I have been at this exposure of giving patterns common among supposedly conservative U.S. foundations which conform with Israeli objectives and not with the American national interests these foundations profess to defend and uphold.

While I have no doubt that the government of Israel can always find ways to make available funds for activities in the United States similar to those of Emerson and his associates, I hope that as a result of the revelations in this study there will be no more funding for such profoundly un-American, even anti-American, activities from at least some of the foundations cited by the authors of this study.

INTRODUCTION

The 1960s was a time for change in America. This period in American history has been referred to as the second American revolution. The Vietnam War, the civil rights movement, the sexual revolution, and the generation gap were all landing heavy blows to America's conscience. America stood resilient against the weakness and instability that can result from the rapid change that fate had thrust upon us. Though the country remained outwardly intact, internally there were many storms brewing that did not reveal their darkened skies, nor rain their troubled waters until years, in fact decades later.

The change of heart that America experienced in the sixties and seventies seemed at the time humbling and purifying. Our young people were questioning the establishment about war, sex, marriage, and gender inequalities. Our minorities were marching in the streets convicting us through their non-violent appeals for justice and equality and frightening us with the utter destruction of whole segments of our major cities, frustrated by our inability to grasp the intensity of their pain and angered by Americas resistance to integration. The majority voice fell silent as another voice shouted from the halls of our universities and our streets, "America must change" the voices cried. And we did, for better or worse.

The imperatives for change in America never ended. There

were periods of ebb and tide. We moved from debates on the use of contraception, to dialogues on premarital sex and concluded the sexual revolution with an increase in homes without fathers, record numbers of women and children in poverty , and an increase in sexually transmitted disease. Americas foreign policies were also reflecting changes as the world around us changed, sometimes predictably, and at other times without warning. Change seemed after the sixties to be more rapid, and severe. Big changes and important events have marked the last 30 years of Americas history.

Among these significant, yet subtle changes was a change in the liberal attitude toward Israel . This change resulted in a split between the more conservative liberals and the more radical liberals who had led the charge against conservatism that put liberals in power, the result of a generation gap and the new voting rights of America's 18 year olds, who rejected establishment conservatism as lacking vision, puritanical and racists. Liberal power and a change in attitude regarding Israel caused red flags to go up in the pro-Israeli liberal camp.

Israel's aggression in the 1967 war in which it occupied much of the territory that is the topic of the contemporary and controversial land for peace process, drew unprecedented condemnation from the left and this shift in position was enough to split the liberals into two camps. Interestingly the pro-Israeli faction took on an entirely new face and name. Neo-conservatives, or the new right made its debut on the American political scene as a venue for moderate liberalism and extreme pro-Israel sentiment.

In an article entitled *Neo-Con Invasion*, Samuel Francis, a nationally syndicated columnist, explains that:

Neo-conservatism appeared as a distinct political identity in the late 1960s, when several establishment liberals and leftists began voicing

14

concern about the radical direction their ideological colleagues were taking on issues such as
the Vietnam war, American foreign policy in
general, and many domestic matters.[1]

Primary among the issues key to the split was Israel. In
1996 Patrick Buchanan, a candidate for the Republican nomination prior to the 1996 presidential election was subjected to
a media attack that shocked conservatives and others.
Buchanan was referred to as a "xenophobe", "nativist," "anti-
Semite" and "Nazi".

According to the *Neo-Con Invasion* article, the intensity of
the media blitz was unlike any media assault launched against
a candidate, liberal or conservative, seeking their parties nomination. Upon close scrutiny by various concerned conservative
groups, Mr. Francis, author of the *Neo-Con Invasion* states that
"it came to be known that this negative media blitz was not
coordinated by the liberal "left" who has always been charged
with "controlling " the media, but was instead launched by
figures from the "new" right, or the "neo-conservatives."

What exactly is a neo-conservative?

According to *The New American*, neo-conservatives are
generally: "anti pornography, anti-homosexuality, anti-drugs,
anti-crime, and anti- the overall permissiveness that began to
flourish with Lyndon Johnson's "Great Society." They are
opposed to the "drug-and-sex-obsessed counter-culture of the
60s, and they generally defend the authority and legitimacy of
traditional morality, religion, and American and Western forms
of government."

In the sixties and seventies these positions would not have
been celebrated. Yet in the 1980s and 90s these claims to conservative values and political views have placed the neo-conservatives in the midst of a conservative revolution of sort, that
recaptured the white house from the Democrats, and put

Ronald Reagan in the presidential seat. This same movement gave Republicans control of the House and the Senate for the first time in more than 20 years.

The neo-conservative ideology centers around a journal entitled, *Commentary* and another, *The Public Interests*, edited by Norman Podhoretz and Irving Krystal respectively. Both editors were known previously as liberal intellectuals.

Originally the mainstream conservative movement embraced the neo-cons. These new allies were welcomed since mainstream conservatives were impressed not only by the academic credentials of many of the neo conservatives, but also by their powerful contacts in the media and universities. Having previously been liberal ideologues and activists, neo-conservatives were also conversant in the liberal dialogue and proved to be very effective in critiquing both liberals and leftists with a credibility that no conservative enjoyed in the same forums. Prior to Reagans' election, perhaps as early as the 1970s ideological conflicts between the two conservative camps began to surface.

In an article written by James Burnham, and published in 1972 in *National Review*, Mr. Burnham, a former Trotskyite who made the transition to what is called "genuine conservatism" wrote:

> While the intellectuals who espoused neo-conservatism might have broken formally with "liberal doctrine" they nevertheless retained in their thinking what might be called "the emotional gestalt of liberalism, the liberal sensitivity and temperament."[2]

The neo-conservatives kept as their heroes Franklin Roosevelt, John Kennedy, Lyndon Johnson and other big government era liberals. Ben Wattenberg and Elliott Abrams, two prominent neo-conservatives broke their ties with organized labor, yet both maintained their liberal attachment to the idea of the welfare state as both "legitimate and inevitable." Irving Kristol, the previously mentioned neo-conservative ideologue and editor of *Commentary*, wrote: " a conservative welfare state ...is perfectly consistent with the neo-conservative perspective."

Old conservative heroes like Barry Goldwater and Howard Taft , were replaced in idealistic writings by neo-conservatives with liberal democrats like Hubert Humphrey, Henry Jackson, and George Marshall.

It is important to mention that as the neo-conservative movement was gaining influence, the United States was itself making a move to the right. Neo-conservatives may have experienced their first major victory strangely enough with the election of President Clinton in 1996. Clinton who is a Democrat, in his 1996 bid for the presidency ran not as a "liberal," but on what could be called, a neo-conservative platform. He ran as a social conservative because various public opinion polls showed that America as a nation was moving right. Frank Newport of the Gallup organization wrote that "America's top priorities in 1996 were the economy and the budget deficit. Only 7% of those polled felt that education was a priority and only 4% felt that welfare reform was a priority."[3] In this same article Mr. Newport observes that both candidates in the 96 election focused on the economy. Dole focused on tax cuts, while Clinton focused on the budget deficit. Interestingly 22% of Dole's supporters agreed with Clinton that the budget deficit was more important than tax cuts by a 3 to 1 margin. To appease this populists move to the right Clinton adopted the neo conservative language and outlook. His campaign speeches focused on domestic issues and family values. He placed little emphasis on the liberal social agenda and issues like abortion and increased government subsidies for social programs. In his foreign policy Clinton remained unconditionally committed to Israel and has maintained his political ties to both the liberal and neo-conservative pro-Israeli camps.

In a presentation entitled *The Challenge to Liberal Modernity*, Dr. Anthony Sullivan of the Earhart Foundation distinguishes the various tribes of conservatism. He says:

> The three tribes are the neo-conservatives, the paleo-conservatives, and the classical liberals. The latter two are potentially friendly to Muslims and to the contemporary Islamic revival...anyone believing that there is any cohesive, homogeneous, "conservatism" in contemporary, post cold war America is making a serious mistake. There are in fact several competing conservatism's.[4]

Mr. Sullivan seems to imply in his remarks that there is a conservative tribe that is obviously anti Muslim and anti Arab.

Dr. Imad ad-Deen Ahmed, president of the Minaret of Freedom Institute in a dialogue sponsored by the United Association for Studies and Research (UASR) on American political movements, offered the following critique of the neo-conservative movement:

> The neo conservatives are among the strident opponents in the West today of Islam and Islamic values, and are ardent Zionists. The neo-conservatives are advocates of the "clash of civilizations" concept. Thirty years ago, they were Henry Jackson Democrats who believed that modern history began with the New Deal and went astray with the student uprisings of the 60's. In simplistic terms, one can say that they were part of the Democratic party until the McGovern campaign, when they broke with the

more liberal element of the Democratic party
over two issues: Viet Nam and Israel.

Dr. Imad ad-Deen identifies neo-cons as the conservative
tribe that is anti-Arab and anti-Muslim.

Neo-Conservative anti-Arab and anti-Muslim bias and
hatred is central to the neo-con foreign policy perspective.
Their understanding of Muslims and Arabs is clouded by negative stereotypes and they use broad generalizations that result
in collective treatment of Muslims and Arabs as so-called "terrorists" and "extremists". This type of stereotyping and the use
of stereotypes upon which to develop policies and responses to
certain situations is similar to Israel's collective punishment of
Arabs and Muslims in Palestine. Collective punishment is to
Israel what anti-Muslim and anti-Arab activities are to neo-
conservatives in the United States.

Both Israeli practices in Palestine and neo-conservative
practices in the United States are racists and contrast the
"democratic" humanitarianism that both display in their writings on American and Israeli patriotism. When one looks
closely at Israel's policies towards Arabs and Muslims and
neo-conservative perspectives and perceptions of Arabs and
Muslims, we find striking and disturbing similarities with
Nazi idealism and the stereotype-driven hatred of Jews that
resulted in the tragedy known as the Holocaust.

The next logical question then is could neo-conservative
biases and hatred of Muslims and Arabs effect the United
States in the same way that Nazi hatred of Jews effected
Germany? There are many political pundits who have drawn
similarities between the erosion of American civil liberties that
has began as a result of the neo-conservative campaign against
Arabs and Muslims in America. Following the Clinton administration's bombing of Sudan and Afghanistan in response to
the American embassy bombings in Kenya and Tanzania,

American subways looked terrifyingly reminiscent of German train stations during the holocaust where the Gestapo patrolled the train stations with dogs, to sniff out Jews. It was later learned that the bombings in Sudan and Afghanistan were based on false and misleading intelligence provided to the State department that led to the bombings and the fear of "terrorists reprisal" that caused America's streets and subways to resemble the streets of Germany in the 1940s. What's tragic is the likelihood that neo-conservative and pro-Israeli activity in America may lead to an elimination of liberty for Muslims and Arabs. Americans of all colors and races are being adversely effected by Steven Emerson's assertion that American civil liberties and our constitution hamper efforts to fight terrorism effectively. Airline profiling, new banking regulations that violate the privacy of American citizens (enacted mostly to track Muslim and Arab money transfers to Palestine), government legislation that limits liberty and free speech for fear of "terrorists" is the result of the neo-conservative campaign against Muslims and Arabs that is, ironically, destroying America and strengthening Israel.

PART I

THE NEO-CONSERVATIVE MOVEMENT AND THE ANTI-MUSLIM AND ARAB CAMPAIGN

FROM COLD WARRIORS TO CRUSADERS

As shown previously the neo-conservative movement sprang from a break between the liberal left and its more conservative members over disputes that revolved around the Vietnam war and Israel. The dissenting members were usually ex-Cold Warriors who had vehemently opposed communism in Russia, though there is little evidence that they were as passionately opposed to communism in China. Nevertheless, they found in the conservative movement a common ideological underpinning for mutual collaboration on certain projects central to the cause of eliminating communism in Russia. Since the fall of communism occurred almost simultaneous to the rise of neo-conservatism, there is a circulating theory that the neo-cons, in an effort to sustain their new adventure into the camps of the right, came up with the ingenious idea of creating a new common enemy. That enemy being Islam and Muslims.

This theory has been very difficult to prove since there is no smoking gun to tie these two camps together on the idea of Islam and Muslims as the "new" enemy. In fact there seems to be more evidence that conservatives are generally opposed to and often offended by the aggressive and sometimes outright racists style of neo-conservatives in their positions against Islam in America. Prominent conservative ideologues like Pat Buchanan and Ronald Reagan, showed in various public statements that they are opposed to American foreign policy that is slavish to Israel. Russell Kirk, one of America's most respected conservative thinkers made a remark in a Heritage Foundation speech that drew the ire of neo-cons. Mr. Kirk opined, "not seldom it has seemed as if some eminent neo conservatives mistook Tel-Aviv for the capital of the United States." This comment was clearly intended to show Mr. Kirk's distaste for the power being demonstrated by the neo-cons over the mainstream conservative positions on Israeli foreign policy which have been called "anti-Semitic." In response to this comment by Mr. Kirk at the Heritage Foundation, a prominent neo-conservative, Midge Dector, who is an appointed member of the Heritage Foundation Board of Trustees and the wife of the neo-conservative ideologue Norman Podhoretz, later attacked Russel Kirk in what has been called a "vitriolic denunciation" calling him an "anti-Semite."

Other conservative establishment organizations and personalities have come under attack by neo-conservatives, and charged with anti-Semitism. This fact alone makes it highly unlikely that the neo-conservative movement has much support among mainstream conservatives in its apparent anti Islam, Muslim and Arab sentiments. Neo conservative attacks on Islam and Muslims seem to follow a pro-Israeli pattern of defamation against Islam. This defamation and vilification may be part of a strategy to eliminate any possibility that a growing Muslim and Arab community in the United States will have any significant amount of political influence.

The issue of immigration is more likely the point of congruence between neo-conservatives and mainstream conservatives than the "cold war" mentality that is blamed. Mainstream conservatives have traditionally held a cautious attitude towards immigration and the supposed threat that it poses to traditional American values and institutions. The old conservatism has served as the ideological custodians of American tradition and sovereignty. Legislation that sought to curtail immigration, not only of Muslims and Arabs, but also of Hispanics, Haitians and others may have been supported by mainstream conservatives, but hidden agendas that called for the use of secret evidence to facilitate deportations under the guise of fighting "terrorism" are clearly the work of pro-Israeli neo-conservatives. If there was collusion with the old right in this respect, this collusion is most likely found in legislative trade-offs that call for some to support others, in order to gain others support. If mainstream conservatives wanted legislation to curtail immigration, the tradeoff may have been to accept the use of secret evidence against the political enemies of the pro-Israeli neo-cons, who are of course Arabs and Muslims, the supposed enemies of Israel. Mr. Francis in his article *New-Con Invasion* showed that neo-cons have little if any interest in American constitutional principles or states rights issues.

THE "CLASH OF CIVILIZATIONS"

A prominent Harvard professor, Dr. Samuel Huntington revived civilizational theories that were popular among 19th and early 20th century intellectuals, but that have long since been discredited. In *The Clash of Civilizations and the Remaking of World Order*, Mr. Huntington cautions that foreign cultures will dissolve the Western world's identity unless we take quick action. He reiterates his pet theme that the main distinctions among peoples are not ideological, political, or economic but cultural. He further asserts that the global order after the dominance of the West, will likely be characterized by multiple competing power centers that reject Western cultural norms and values. Huntington, identifies Islam as one of the main enemies of the West.[1]

Huntington's theory has been discredited for its reductionism.[2] However, its simplicity appeals in particular to neo-conservatives seeking scholarly justification for their programs, and who consider Huntington's work a vindication for their anti-Arab and Muslim tendencies.

THE ZIONIST CONNECTION

Civilizational hypothesis of a clash between Western and Islamic civilizations also enjoy wide support among American hard-line defenders of Israel.[3] In a lecture at Georgetown University on April 15, 1997, Rivka Yadlin, Professor at the Hebrew University of Jerusalem excoriated Muslim culture of its inability for dialogue with the West.

> Dialogue, to state the obvious, is beyond the pale of Islamist reformers. But not only theirs. Mainstream intellectual Islamdom is just as adamant in foreclosing not only dialogue, but even a depiction or foreshadowing of an understanding.

And further:

> The Islamic voice ... speaks of tension verging on polarization; of distaste, often touching on abhorrence; of confrontation, both defensive and aggressive. There is a definite visceral demarcation between self and others, we and them,

Muslims and the West; the latter bearing the
onus of its ascendancy, whether in past Colonial
control, or present scientific supremacy. [4]

While the neo-conservatives of the Christian Coalition and
the Israeli lobby would seem to have little in common religiously or ideologically, their goals converge with regard to
their advocacy of U.S. support for Israel as the outpost of
Western civilization against the civilization of Islam. Jerry
Falwell, leader of the religious fundamentalist wing of the
coalition movement known as the "Moral Majority," said that
"To stand against Israel is to stand against God," and that
"Jews have a God-Given Right to the Land," and that "God has
raised up America in these last days for the cause of world
evangelization and for the protection of his people the Jews. I
don't think America has any other right or reason for existence
other than those two purposes."[5]

STRATEGIC CONVERGENCE

The strategic convergence of the neo-conservatives and
elements of the Christian Coalition and the Israeli lobby on the
defense of Western civilization has given "terrorism/funda-
mentalism experts and entrepreneurs " like Steven Emerson
and Khalid Duran publicity in the media. This is due to the
neo-cons vast influence with the liberal media. Although neo-
cons do not consider themselves "liberals" as shown in previous discussion they have never split ideologically with the left
on any substantive issues other than Viet Nam and Israel.
Steven Emerson casts himself in his writings as a neo conservative even though most of his career prior to becoming a journalists was spent as a liberal political operative.

In fact, many of the mainstream conservative publications

like the *National Review, The American Spectator,* and the *Wall Street Journal* came under the sway of neo-cons due to their growing power over mainstream conservatives, and their gain in influence over conservative think tanks and foundations. These conservative foundations, funded mostly by wealthy conservative families to serve philanthropic goals, were first taken over administratively by the neo-conservatives. These administrative powers were used to re-direct funds from mainstream conservative organizations to the neo-con establishments that include organizations like Heritage Foundation. The primary mechanism for the re-direction of conservative money to neo conservative organizations is an organization called the Philanthropic Roundtable that was established in 1987 by Leslie Lenkowsky. Lenkowsky, announcing the new funding policy of the neo-conservative "Philanthropic Roundtable" said, "We will encourage foundations to think more about how they can achieve their objectives and to look more closely at what groups they support and what they really are accomplishing...any organization with the word "liberty" or "conservative" in its name will not be automatically funded."

The first organizations to be cut from the lists for funding according to the article *Neo Con Invasion,* were the Rockford Institute and The John Birch Society, two of the most prominent mainstream conservative organizations. Both were charged with anti-Semitism. The late M.E. Bradford was another prominent causality of the neo-conservative takeover of the conservative trusts and foundations. Mr. Bradford was a professor of English at the University of Dallas and a leading conservative ideologue. He was nominated for appointment as the head of the National Endowment for the Humanities, an organization that controls the flow of federal money to scholarships in the humanities. His rival was William J. Bennett , who was the Director of the National Humanities Center at the University of

North Carolina at Chapel Hill. Bennet has a liberal background that is demonstrated in his various writings. The story goes that since Bennett, who was the obvious choice of the neo-conservatives, lacked comparable credentials, or experience with Bradford, Bradford was subjected to a smear campaign in which he was accused of advocating slavery and praising Adolph Hitler. A secret document circulated through the White House that made these unsubstantiated charges frightened the Reagan Administration into denying Bradford the appointment.

Other benefactors of neo-con support have been Frank Gaffney's ultra-right Center for Security Policy, which receives funding from the defense industry (General Dynamics, Lockheed Martin, Northrop), and the conservative Bradley, Olin, Scaife, Smith Richardson, and Heritage Foundations. It also serves "as a gathering point for neo-conservative Jews seeking to undermine efforts ... to make peace with the P.L.O."[6] The Center receives endorsement of its views from the neo conservative and pro Israeli journal *Commentary*. Its board of advisers includes hard-line supporters of Israel such as former AIPAC director Morris J. Amitay. Gaffney also receives funding from conservative pro-Israeli foundations such as the Irving I. Moskowitz Foundation ($75,000 in 1995) for his lobbying efforts against deploying U.S. troops in the Golan Heights, because this would allegedly expose American lives to terrorist actions.[7]

THE SPONSORS

The neo-conservative crusade against so-called "alien civilizations besieging the Western world" is funded by a small number of wealthy conservative foundations. The Washington, D.C. based watchdog organization People for the American Way, a leftist organization that was founded to advance a liberal media campaign against conservatives, has shown in its detailed study, *Buying a Movement: Right-Wing Foundations and American Politics*[8] that a handful of foundations provide the bulk of money for conservative think tanks, professors, and journalists. These academicians and journalists give intellectual credence to the agenda of the neo-cons referred to generically by the authors as the " New Right."

Most of these wealthy foundations are interlocking.

• The Lynde and Harry Bradley Foundation has close ties to the right-wing and pro-Israeli journals *National Review*, and the *American Spectator*.[9]

• The neo-conservative and pro-Israeli journals *Commentary*, and *Public Interest* receive Olin grants.

• Richard Mellon Scaife bankrolls the Sarah Scaife Foundation, the Carthage Foundation, and the Allegheny Foundation which provide grants for the Heritage Foundation, the libertarian Cato Institute and the Center for Strategic and International Studies (CSIS).

Together with the Smith Richardson Foundation, the Bradley, Olin, and Scaife Foundations are often referred to as the "four sisters of conservative philanthropy."[10]

Among the major conservative foundations, one must also mention the

• Adolph Coors Foundation which also supports the above conservative think tanks, displays an openly anti-minorities funding pattern, and maintains close relations with the religious right.

• The Koch Family Foundation, which show similar funding patterns for conservative and libertarian causes.[11]

THE RECIPIENTS: BUYING SCHOLARLY JUSTIFICATION

Together with a large number of smaller foundations and individual donors, the six big foundations promote an agenda that many believe is inimical to racial integration and that conjures up a picture of the United States as a country under siege. This in turn could create an environment that is ripe for the proliferation of anti Muslim and anti Arab sentiments, causing Islam to be cast falsely as a "Trojan Horse" and a threat to American culture and security. These funding patterns are not a smoking gun. Their mention here is not intended to imply that these funding institutions are anti-Arab or anti-Muslim. These funding patterns do indicate that the administrative takeover of conservative philanthropy by neo conservatives could seriously effect the political discourse and environment in America, causing public opinion and policy to reflect neo conservative antagonism towards Muslims and Arabs. A brief look at some of the individual recipients of money from conservative foundations reveals a pattern of collusion between neo conservatives and pro-Israeli organizations.

Among the most prominent recipients are the adversaries of multiculturalism such as the late Allan Bloom, Dinesh D'Souza, and Charles Murray, all of whom deplore the loss of the United States' identity and moral cohesion due to attempts to integrate "alien cultures" incompatible with what they consider genuinely Western values.

• Allan Bloom, who received $3.6 million from Olin, headed the University of Chicago's John M. Olin Center for Inquiry into the Theory and Practice of Democracy.[12] In *The Closing of the American Mind*, Bloom deplores the decline of the teaching of Western civilization in the United States since the 1960s, and laments the rise of multiculturalism, which could also include religious pluralism since religious idealism significantly impacts cultural development and norms.

NEO-CONSERVATIVE FOUNDATIONS AND THE "CLASH OF CIVILIZATIONS"

While imaginary threats like Steven Emerson's "International Islamic terrorists network" based in the United States constitute the main target of the conservative movement, dangers from the outside receive considerable attention. Not surprisingly, Samuel Huntington's Program on National Security Affairs received $200,000 from Bradley in 1990, and Olin allegedly awarded Huntington $2.5 million.[13] An overview of the funding patterns of the major foundations in recent years reveals their preoccupation with matters of national security.[14] This is not in and of itself anti-Muslim or anti-Arab. Only when imaginary threats like those created by Emerson and Huntington are accepted as "the" threats to American security does this funding become suspect.

(1) A partial list of the funding of conservative institutions and academic programs concerned with U.S. security policy looked as follows (1994):

The Sarah Scaife Foundation gave
- $125,000 to Frank Gaffney's Center for Security Policy
- $470,000 to the Center for Strategic and International Studies (CSIS) in Washington, D.C.
- $420,000 to the Institute for Foreign Policy Analysis in Cambridge, MA
- $91,000 to the Southwest Missouri State University Foundation, Center for Defense and Strategic Studies in Springfield, MO
- $18,000 to the University of Cincinnati for the National Security Education Seminar
- $250,000 to the University of Virginia Law School, Center for National Security Law.

30

Richard M. Scaife's Carthage Foundation, gave
- $125,000 to the Center for Security Policy
- $100,000 to the Institute for Foreign Policy Analysis
- $50,000 to the American Defense Institute in Washington, D.C.
- $35,000 to the United States Global Strategy Council in Washington, D.C.

The Olin Foundation gave
- $170,000 to the Academy Research and Development Institute, Colorado Springs, for the John M. Olin Program in National Security Affairs
- $170,000 to the Association of Graduates of the United States Military Academy, West Point for the John M. Olin Program in National Security Affairs
- $460,368 to Harvard University, Center for International Affairs, for the John M. Olin Institute for Strategic Studies
- $32,717 to Harvard University, Center for International Affairs, for the John M. Olin Faculty Fellowship
- $50,000 to the Johns Hopkins University, School of Advanced International Studies, for study groups on ethnic conflict and on changes in American culture and U.S. foreign policy.

The Lynde and Harry Bradley Foundation gave
- $100,000 to Harvard University, Center for International Affairs, for its program on national security
- $163,054 to the Johns Hopkins University, School of Advanced International Studies, for its program on Russian and American national security policymaking
- $150,000 to the Johns Hopkins University, School of Advanced International Studies, for teaching and research activities of Strategic Studies Program
- $225,000 to the National Strategy Information Center

In 1990 Bradley gave:
- $200,000 to Harvard University, Center for International Affairs, for a program on National Security Affairs under the direction of Samuel Huntington

Smith Richardson gave:
- $70,000 to CSIS, $20,000 of which for a project on American Foreign Policy into the 21st Century
- $100,000 to Harvard University, for Four Challenges to American Security project
- $12,000 to Johns Hopkins University, Foreign Policy Institute-SAIS, for research, End of the Cold War and the Future of American Foreign Policy
- $144,000 to the National Strategy Information Center, Washington, D.C., for Challenges from Emerging Global Ungovernability project
- $60,995 to Ohio State University, for American Defense Annual
- $158,000 to Princeton University, for research program in International Security
- $110,000 to the United States Committee of the International Institute for Strategic Studies, Washington, D.C., for Strategic Comments
- $24,000 to Yale University, Cowles Foundation for Research in Economics, for seminar in defense analysis and arms control methodology

(2) Conservative institutions and individuals mainly concerned with the danger of international terrorism, and the safety of Israel received funding from the following sources:

The pro-Israeli and anti-Arab Foreign Policy Research Institute in Philadelphia, directed by Daniel Pipes, received

money from
Scaife:

- $75,000 (1994) for general operating support
- $75,000 (1993) for general operating support
- $75,000 (1992) for general operating support
- $75,000 (1991) for general operating support
- $75,000 (1990) for general operating support

Bradley:

- $100,000 (1994) for research on Islam
- $18,950 (1993) for book project on Foreign Service
- $125,000 (1993) for research on threats to U.S. security
- $18,950 (1992) for book project on Foreign Service
- $77,000 (1992) for research on transition from totalitarianism to democracy
- $154,000 (1990) for research on future of Communist states

Olin:

- $20,000 (1993) for completion of book *Mohammed's Army: The Rise of Islamic Fundamentalism* (by Steven Abram Emerson)
- $40,000 (1990) for books on poverty and economic development in the Third World

Smith Richardson:

- $91,086 (1994) for Kazakhstan project
- $100,000 (1993)
- $100,000 (1992) for media outreach and publications

The recently opened Institute for International Studies in Washington, D.C., which promotes the study in international Islamic fundamentalist movements, and publishes Khálid Durán's journal *TransState Islam* received substantial funding from

Bradley:
- $150,000 (1994) for research on transnational Islam

Olin:
- $10,000 (1993)

Smith Richardson:
- $75,000 (1994) for Nonproliferation Education Center

William H. Donner Foundation:
- $250,000 (1994) for Nonproliferation Education Center

(3) In addition to sponsoring institutions, conservative foundations, fund writing and film projects that deal with the dangers emanating from non-Western cultures.

Smith Richardson provided
- $222,000 to the National Defense University foundation for writing a historical overview on "Managing the Peace" (1992-94)
- $25,000 to the National Strategy Information Center for *Contending Visions* (1994).
- $100,000 to the Institute for Democracy in Eastern Europe, New York, for *Uncaptive Minds* (1994)
- $53,290 for a book on *Islam, Democracy and Market Development* (1994)

Bradley gave
- $77,000 to George Washington University for a book on the U.S. foreign service during the Cold War (1993)
- $200,000 to Pacem Productions, Los Angeles, for a documentary film on the history of Communist movements (1993-94)

- • $15,000 to the Galex Foundation for the production of the documentary Democracy and Islam (1993)
- • $100,000 to the Corporation for Public Broadcasting for a documentary on Islam and terrorism (1994), later titled *Jihad in America* and produced by Steven Abram Emerson, with the assistance of Khálid Durán of the Foreign Policy Research Institute (1994)

Olin gave
- • Eliot Abrams $40,000 for a book on American Foreign policy in the Post-Cold War era (1994)
- • The Foreign Policy Research Institute 20,000 for the completion of a book on *Mohammed's Army: The Rise of Islamic Fundamentalism* by Steven Abram Emerson (1993)

Books on International Relations Sponsored by Neo-Conservatives

A detailed analysis of works on international relations sponsored by neo-conservative foundations would go beyond the scope of this study. For our purposes, a brief overview of the funding of a number of popular works and films, and the interaction between like-minded scholars, and journalists will suffice.

- • Uri Ra'anan, Robert L. Pfaltzgraff, Jr., and Richard H. Shultz edited *Hydra of Carnage: The International Linkages of Terrorism and Other Low-Intensity Operations*,[15] which analyzes a theoretical international terrorist network supposedly sponsored by the Soviet Union in cooperation with certain Muslim and Arab governments. The book was funded by the International Security Studies Program of the Fletcher School for Law and Diplomacy at Tufts, which from its inception was funded by the Sarah Scaife Foundation.
- • With a grant from the Earhart Foundation, Walter Laqueur wrote his *The Age of Terrorism*[16] while the Soviet Union

was still intact. Laqueur was born in Israel, maintains close ties with the Jaffee Center, the Center for Strategic and International Studies (CSIS), which is heavily funded by the above-mentioned conservative foundations, and the Jewish Institute for National Security Affairs, which has close ties to the Israeli government. The book blames the Soviet Union, and its proxies Libya, Syria, Iran and others for anti-Western terrorism, and emphasizes that Israel only engages in counter-terrorism in retaliation for terrorist acts by Palestinian groups.[17]

• Robert Satloff, the executive director of the pro-Israeli Washington Institute for Near East Policy (WINEP), a spin-off of AIPAC, acknowledged the Bradley Foundation for funding his edited work *The Politics of Change in the Middle East.*[18]

• Travel writer Robert Kaplan, who rose to fame with his pro-Israeli book *The Arabists*, received funding from numerous conservative foundations, and enjoys the intellectual support of pro-Israeli think tanks. In a very readable style, Kaplan ceaselessly reiterates that chaos and decay reigns in Third World countries, and that moral corruption endangers the Western world. Like Huntington, Kaplan uses 18th-century theories of the rise and fall of Empires as his template to analyze current developments.[19] In an article for the *Atlantic Monthly*, he presaged the gradual fragmentation of Mexico and the United States into different regional entities that will develop novel modes of interaction beyond today's national boundaries.[20] Like Huntington and the "terrorism experts" discussed below, Kaplan aims to stir up fear of unpredictable and irrational forces lurking in the developing world, against which the United States is unable to defend itself. Moreover, by developing the scenario of the United States' impending loss of territorial cohesion, he gives ammunition to the neo conservatives who advocate tough measures to prevent the erosion of the country's identity through immigration, multiculturalism.

Kaplan owes much of his funding and intellectual support to neo-conservative and pro-Israeli sources:

• His book *Soldiers of God: With the Mujahidin in Afghanistan*[21] was funded by the Olin Foundation and the Institute for Educational Affairs, which receives over $50,000 annually from Olin and Smith Richardson.

• *Surrender or Starve: The Wars Behind the Famine*[22] also received a grant from the Institute for Educational Affairs.

• *Balkan Ghosts: A Journey Through History*[23] was funded by the Madison Center for Educational Affairs, which in 1994 received $210,000 from the Bradley Foundation, $100,000 from Olin and Scaife respectively, and $50,000 from Smith Richardson. Daniel Pipes, former director of the Foreign Policy Research Institute advised Kaplan in writing this book.

• *To the Ends of the Earth: A Journey at the Dawn of the 21st Century*[24] enjoyed the financial support of the Foreign Policy Research Institute, Samuel Huntington's Olin Institute for Strategic Studies (Harvard). Kaplan, moreover, received advise and research support from Yehuda Mirsky and Harvey Sicherman from WINEP.

• *The Arabists: The Romance of an American Elite*[25] was funded by the Bradley Foundation, with the money administered by the Foreign Policy Research Institute. Notorious anti-Muslim demagogue and pro-Zionist Daniel Pipes contributed his expertise. Kaplan reciprocated by choosing one of Pipes' books for his bibliography, and by quoting Steven Emerson,[26] who shares Pipes' world view. Reviewers pointed out that *The Arabists* lacks analytical rigor, and pointlessly indulges in incriminating State Department officials for their allegedly "pro-Arab" stance. This did not prevent Steven Emerson from calling the book "a carefully balanced and fascinating glimpse into the nexus between Foggy Bottom and the Middle East."[27]

• James Phillips of the neo-conservative Heritage Foundation published a paper in which he argued that Middle

Eastern fundamentalist terrorists "often are supported by networks of radical Islamic activists who live in Muslim communities in the West."[28] He argued that "motivated by apocalyptic zeal, and not sober political calculations, they pose a mortal
danger to U.S. citizens all around the world." Phillips advises
that the United States has to remain tough in the face of this
challenge, and use diplomatic measures coupled with military
force against the supporters of fundamentalists, in particular
Iran, Iraq, and Sudan. Phillips' sources are conservative U.S.
and Israeli journalists, including Steven Emerson. Heritage has
long been known for its anti-Soviet politics, and in the past
published numerous studies "proving" the existence of a
Soviet-sponsored terror network.[29] Now it appears that the
Heritage think tank follows the lead of neo-conservative pro-
Israelis and fundamentalist American Christians, and fabri-
cates scholarly justifications for the existence of a global
Islamic threat.

It is obvious that there exists a cooperation between neo-
conservative pro Israeli scholars and journalists, and neo-conservative, pro- Israeli institutions, all of which strive to fabri-
cate a scholarly foundation that "proves" mounting dangers
for the United States and Israel emanating from non-Western
civilizations in general and from Islam in particular.

TERRORISM, FUNDAMENTALISM AND THE THESIS OF THE DECLINE OF THE UNITED STATES

The terrorism scare in the United States reached its peak in
the early 1980s as a reaction to the Iran hostage crisis of (1979-
80). Without exception, the same elements discussed by the
"terrorism experts" during the Reagan administration can be
found in the publications of today's "fundamentalism experts."

One of the events inaugurating the era of the terrorism scare was a conference in July 1979 in Jerusalem organized by the Jonathan Institute, founded by Benjamin Netanyahu in the same year.[30] From its inception, the Institute promoted the theory that the Palestinian Liberation Organization (PLO) was a terrorist organization, sponsored by the Soviet Union, and responsible for almost every act of terrorism anywhere in the world. Among the participants were American neo-conservative journalists, and experts such as George Bush, Ray Cline, Midge Decter, Norman Podhoretz, George Will and Claire Sterling. A follow-up conference five years later (June 1984) in Washington, D.C., assembled equally illustrious analysts and politicians. The contributions of the 1984 conference were edited by Benjamin Netanyahu in *Terrorism: How the West Can Win*,[31] and detail the dimensions of threat to Western civilization by Soviet-sponsored terrorist organizations. Note that Zionists continue to utilize the Soviet theme as a common enemy of all Americans, and as a point of congruence between Zionism and American conservatism.

The 1979 conference inspired journalist Claire Sterling to write her bestseller *The Terror Network*,[32] which relied mainly on dubious sources, and unsubstantiated speculations, but which nevertheless became popular among high ranking politicians in the Reagan administration.[33] Sterling argued that a network of international terrorists, controlled and directed by the Soviet Union, was trying to undermine western democracies. The author conceded that the Soviets lacked absolute control over such movements, but she asserted that they all "come to see themselves as elite battalions in a worldwide Army of Communist Combat."[34] A few years later, the renowned Orientalist and scholar-turned-propagandist Bernard Lewis published "The Roots of Muslim Rage," in *The Atlantic Monthly* (September 1990), arguing that Islam as a religion is hostile to Western civilization.

In the post-Cold War era, the arguments expounded by the anti-Soviet terrorism experts have changed very little. As Hermann and O'Sullivan explain, "terrorism experts" continue to reiterate the arguments from the Cold War era:[35]

- The West is an innocent target and victim of terrorism.
- The West only reacts to terrorism, and never commits acts of terrorism itself.
- Terrorists intend to spread fear, and fail to adhere to civilized norms of conduct.
- Terrorists hate democracies on principle.
- Democracies are vulnerable, and cannot have difficulty defending themselves against terrorists who take advantage of the freedoms that they do not enjoy in their countries of origins.
- There exists some kind of global conspiracy intend to destroy the Western democratic systems.

Linkage of Fear: Communism Equals Terrorism, Equals Muslim Fundamentalism

Today, Muslim fundamentalism is characterized by almost the exact same attributes as the "Communist-sponsored" terrorists of the past. In a critique of the "liberal" approach to Islamic fundamentalism, *Daniel Pipes*, an unabashedly pro-Likud,[36] anti-Islamic scholar-turned-propagandist, the former director of the neo-conservative Foreign Policy Institute, and editor of *Middle East Quarterly*,[37] aptly summarized the continuity between yesterday's liberal Cold Warriors, and today's anti-fundamentalists. Pipes argues that:

> ... fundamentalists challenge the West more profoundly than Communists did and do ... (*sic!*). The latter disagree with our politics but not with our whole view of the world .... In contrast, fundamentalist Muslims despise our

40

whole way of life, including the way we dress, mate, and pray.[38]

As a result,

> [t]he Western confrontation with fundamentalist Islam has in some ways come to resemble the great ideological battle of the twentieth century, that between Marxism-Leninism and liberal democracy.[39]

Pipes carefully explains how the neo-conservatives who are former liberals challenge their liberal counterparts. The following points are paradigmatic for the discourse of the neo-conservative on religious fundamentalism.

- Instead of looking at fundamentalism as an expression of social grievances, the neo-conservative sees radical utopian ideology as "a powerful force in itself."[40]
- Instead of promoting economic growth and social equality, the Right blames ambitious fundamentalist intellectuals, who "must be battled and defeated."
- Instead of conceding that Western imperialism contributed to the rise of fundamentalism, the neo-conservative holds that the real culprits are the "tyrants" in the Muslim world.
- Instead of acknowledging that there are a wide variety of indigenous sources for fundamentalist movements, the neo-conservative believes that "Tehran administers a network akin to an Islamist Comintern, making its role today not that different from Moscow's then."[41]
- Instead of distinguishing between moderate and radical fundamentalists, neo-conservatives perceive no major difference, and "tend to lump most Communists and fundamentalists together."

- Instead of realizing that Muslims are mainly concerned with their own societies, the neo-conservative Zionists argue that they "are deeply anti-Western and invariably target the West [...] to challenge the predominance of modern, Western civilization.

- Instead of perceiving constructive elements in Islamic discourse, neo-conservatives argue that "like Communism, fundamentalism has to end up in the dustbin of history."

- Instead of understanding that Islamic fundamentalism poses no threat to the West, neo-conservatives insists that the Christian West, including Russia, has to hold "the frontier of Christendom against its common enemy, the Muslim world."

- Instead of engaging in constructive dialogue with Islamic fundamentalists, neo-conservatives assert that containment and rollback are still necessary, and that "we should show not empathy but resolve, not good will but will power", enforced by the military.[2]

Pipes' perception of siege goes beyond alien cultures threatening the United States. He accuses "liberals" of supporting the cause of fundamentalism, and misleading the public. He concludes that the Left's elitist and "soft" approach to fundamentalism has become the hegemonic discourse in the United States, and that only the patriotic actions of the neo-conservative can save the country from the fundamentalists' rage. This is the grand strategy at its best; to target and demonize the left and distract attention from the Clinton administration and its pro-Israel policies, while utilizing the growing popularity of conservative idealism in America to shape popular opinion on certain issues that are compatible. This strategy allows optimum exploitation of both the right and left by pro-Israel propagandist.

> On the other side stand nothing but a handful of
> scholars, some commentators and politicians, and
> the great common sense of the American common
> people. Americans know an opponent when they
> see him, and they are not fooled by the Left's
> fancy arguments. That common sense prevailed
> in the Cold War and no doubt will suffice yet
> again to overcome the follies of the New Class.[43]

Pipes is mistaken to conclude that it is the "fancy arguments" or elitist discourse of liberals that shapes public opinion. In reality, it is the skillful manipulation of the so-called
"common sense" of the uninformed public, and the evocation
of deep-rooted but unsubstantiated fears for political purposes
that amount to what is commonly called demagoguery. By
decontextualizing modern fundamentalist movements, Pipes
offers nothing but the stale slogans of the Cold War in response
to the sophisticated (in his words "fancy") scholarly analyses
that see Muslim fundamentalist movements as a response to
local conditions, and suggest responses appropriate to their
social, historical, and political context.[44] Again we must keep in
mind that this is an opportunistic argument contrived to
extend neo-conservative Zionism into the mainstream
American political discourse.

Similar to the above article, Pipes' new book, *The Hidden
Hand: Middle East Fear of Conspiracy*,[45] funded by the Smith
Richardson Foundation, is a concatenation of statements by
fundamentalists quoted out of context, and intended to
"prove" that Arabs and Muslims cannot be trusted because
they believe that there is a Western conspiracy against them.
Predictably, pro-zionist journalists and intellectuals supported
Pipes compiling his book. Among them were Charles
Krauthammer and Patrick Clawson, who provided counsel;
Bernard Lewis, who read the manuscript; as well as Nissim

Rejwan, Barry Rubin and Hilal Khashan, who supplied information. All former liberals of the Viet Nam era.

Another book by Pipes shows similar patterns. *The Rushdie Affair: The Novel, the Ayatollah, and the West* was written under the auspices of the Foreign Policy Research Institute. Bernard Lewis and Khálid Durán provided clippings and read the manuscript, and Steven Emerson provided counsel.[46]

Today, the dominant discourse on fundamentalism hinges on semi-truths, and distortions similar to the ones presented above. Besides Pipes, the best-known proponents of the neocons approach to fundamentalism are Steven Emerson and Khálid Durán, the collaborators of the documentary *Jihad in America*. Since it aired on PBS in 1994, numerous neo-conservative imitators have propagated the threat of fundamentalism, and it is to be expected that more propagandists and demagogues will manipulate the "common sense" of the American public for their own goals, and these propagandists will include liberals represented by Madeline Albright, Sandy Berger, and William Cohen.

A *fter PBS aired the documentary **Jihad in***
America: An Investigation of Islamic
Extremists Activities in the United States on
November 21, 1994, the image of Muslims por-
trayed in this production has come to dominate pub-
lic discourse, and spawned a number of pseudo-
scholarly productions intended to show that the U.S.
is under siege by an evil and unpredictable force.
Newspapers and T. V. networks uncritically reiterate
such fears, and Congress introduced the anti-terror-
ism legislation which to a large extent relied on evi-
dence presented by these so-called experts.

In their quest to capitalize on American fear
through the vilification of an American minority,
these terrorism entrepreneurs employ a strategy of
half truths and propaganda, to divide our country
along racial and religious lines by emphasizing that
the sole motive of " Muslim terrorists" is their unbri-
dled hatred of the West. American Muslims have
become the victims of this reductionists message since
they are the primary voices of activism and resis-
tance against the continued Israeli occupation of
Palestine, and Zionists hegemony in the Muslim
world.

PART II

STEVEN EMERSON

JIHAD in America

Jihad in America represents only one aspect of a very complex media campaign launched by pro-Israeli neo-conservatives in the United States. It was preceded by a series of anti-Muslim and Arab opinion pieces written by leading propagandists. Joel Greenberg, Judith Miller, Yossef Bodansky, and others laid the foundation upon which *Jihad in America* poised itself as a credible work.

One of the primary objectives of this media campaign was to stop the international condemnation of Israel that had resulted from Rabin's decision to round up and expel 400 Palestinian professionals from their homes and exile them to Lebanon as punishment for their legal, though undesirable, anti-Israel political activism in the West Bank and Gaza. In a special report to the *New York Times*, Paul Lewis wrote, "In a strongly worded rebuke backed by the United States, the U.N. Security Council voted unanimously on Friday night to condemn Israel for deporting about 400 Palestinians from the occupied territories."[1] In another *New York Times* special report, Clyde Haberman reported on the highest Palestinian death toll in a single day, resulting from an Israeli military attack on

47

Palestinian civilians who had gotten out of hand while struggling to get food after a week long curfew had been lifted that prevented the people from buying food. Among those killed was an 8 year old girl.[2] On December 19th another article appeared, this one written by Ali Jaber and published by *The Times Saturday*. In this article Mr. Jaber states that "the decision to deport the group was attacked by the European community, which issued a statement through the British presidency. The EC said that Israel had breached international law and expressed regret that pleas for clemency have been ignored."[3]

The Fourth Geneva Convention Article 49 clearly states that "individual or mass forcible transfers, as well as deportations of protected persons from occupied territory to the territory of the occupying power or to that of any other country, occupied or not, are prohibited, regardless of their motive." Israel claimed that since the Geneva Convention had never been incorporated into Israeli law, Israel was not compelled to abide by the Convention and therefore could not be in breech of the law.

Israel saw itself losing the unquestioning international support and sympathy to which it had become accustomed. Israeli soldiers had killed thousands of Palestinian civilians throughout its years of occupation in Palestine,[4] yet the illegal expulsion of these Hamas activists threatened Israel's American support and the support of the international communities because the expulsion threatened the Middle East peace talks.[5] A series of anti-Israel articles began to appear in the Western media, signaling an end to unconditional Western support of Israeli aggression in the occupied territories and an end to passionate attachments that Israel forged with the Western world.[6] Ironically the 1949 Geneva Convention articles, which Israel now breached without conscience, are international laws that came into being as a result of the Holocaust and the world's determination to prevent such a tragedy from ever happening again.

Using its propaganda network in the American media, Israel struck back in an intense media attack against Hamas and Islamic activism. Israel was determined to vilify the Hamas movement and all Islamic reform and resistance movements, labeling them "terrorist," even though the Fourth Geneva Convention clearly protects the rights of any indigenous people to use military force in resisting foreign occupation of their land. In an effort to eliminate any sympathy that Hamas might have garnered as a result of the expulsions, the pro-Israeli and neo-conservative media machine went into full gear, creating and propagating fictitious but frightening stories about Islamic militants hiding in America, waiting to conduct terrorist operations against the United States.

Many suspect that pro-Israeli agents went even further than mere propaganda. According to an article written by Joseph Brewda, a regular contributor to the *Executive Intelligence Review (EIR)*, Israeli president Chaim Herzog made the first ever visit of an Israeli president to Britain. There he announced that Israel was involved in a major battle against Iranian controlled Islamic fundamentalism. Herzog added, according to Brewda, "It's true that that there's no Soviet Union now threatening, but there are all sorts of lunatic states like Iran and Iraq and so forth, which could upset the whole balance in the world." Two days later a car bomb exploded in the underground garage of the World Trade Center building in New York City killing six people and injuring hundreds. Mr. Brewda states that in the World Trade Center case the media relied upon Israeli or Israeli linked "experts" to get the story. Among these so-called "experts" were Uri Dan, the biographer of Ariel Sharon. Mr. Dan was the first to suggest that the World Trade Center bombing was carried out by Islamic extremists. The tone of the investigation was set and the public perception of the bombing was shaped through the media by Wolf Blitzer, formerly of the Jerusalem Post but now employed by Cable News Network; Steven Emerson; Robert Friedman, who criticizes the Israeli government using Israeli intelligence reports; Roy Godson, the liaison between Israel and the United States in the Iran-Contra affair; and the U.S. based Israeli "expert" Avigdur Haselkorn. A *Village Voice* expose charged that the Mossad was actually linked to the World Trade Center bombing.[7] It was the World Trade Center bombing that gave Emerson and others the credibility they needed to make policy recommendations that mobilized large sums of American personnel and taxpayer money in support of the Israeli battle to maintain its occupation of Palestine. It wasn't until the Oklahoma City bombing that Emerson undid himself by claiming that the bombing was the work of an "Islamic terrorists" network in America.[8]   Shortly after Emerson made these remarks, a white American male suspect was arrested and subsequently convicted of the bombing. Muslims had questioned the Justice Department investigation prior to the suspect's conviction. It was difficult to believe that the Justice Department never had a clue that could have vindicated Muslims prior to the McVeigh conviction and before the Oklahoma backlash against Muslims. This backlash resulted in the death of an infant and the humiliation and fear of many other innocent people. Neither the Justice Department nor Emerson have ever offered an apology for this tragedy, which many believe was actually an anticipated and possibly welcomed reaction. How could Emerson have known so much about the character of the bombing prior to the investigation?

In 1993 Joel Greenberg wrote in the *New York Times* that Israeli security officials believe Hamas had moved its main command structure to the United States after repeated arrests of its leaders in the occupied territories. Greenberg charged that "Hamas operatives in the United States exercise regional command and control of the West bank and Gaza strip, order guerrilla attacks, and receive reports from the occupied territories."[9] The report went on further to say that it was the Hamas movement that Israel was seeking to eliminate in the Palestinian expulsions. In making this assertion, the Israeli propagandists successfully frightened the American people and stimulated an almost panicked response from law and policy makers, which have resulted in the most serious infringements on civil liberties in American history.[10]

On November 21, 1994, PBS aired the documentary *Jihad in America*, the work of Steven Emerson and Khálid Durán. This film roused a storm of protest by American Muslims and Arab-Americans. Funded by the Bradley and Carthage Foundations,[11] *Jihad* hammers away the message that the United States has been infiltrated by fundamentalist radicals who ruthlessly exploit the freedoms granted to them by their democratic host. Guided by their innate anti-Semitism and unbridled hate for anything western, their ultimate goal, according to Emerson, is "to establish an Islamic empire"[12] that includes the United States." Their strategy to achieve this goal is to strike at their host, and to inflict maximum damage to Israel.

The film is a compilation of sound bites and interviews with members of unrelated movements taken out of context. Its implicit aim is to create fear of Muslim "savages" plotting their evil plans within the United States in "numerous command centers and communication posts." *Jihad* conveys the message that "hampered by Constitutional constraints, U.S. law enforcement will have difficulty preventing the nation from becoming a war front." "As the activities of Muslim radicals expand in the United States, future attacks seem inevitable."

The film's sources are mainly interviews with former U.S. intelligence officials and members of various Muslim organizations. Emerson takes their rhetoric at face value without trying to validate their statements. He interprets statements such as "The world today is arbitrarily ruled by Jews and

Christians" (Abdullah Azzam), or "Our problems are solved in the trenches fighting, not in the hotels around tables", (Tamim al-Adnani) as expressions of general hatred for the West, Christianity and Judaism. Emerson fails to realize that such statements reflect the struggle of oppressed groups against the Israeli occupation of the West Bank and Gaza or the Soviet invasion of Afghanistan and were never made in reference to any antagonism toward the West.

Among the Islamic organizations singled out in the film are Hezbollah and Hamas, both of which fight for the liberation of Israeli-occupied land. Whatever their completely legal fundraising and recruiting activities in the United States are, they have never been responsible for any illegal activity on U.S. soil. Their actions in South Lebanon and the Occupied Territories (the West Bank and Gaza Strip) are the outcome of decades of Israeli oppression, and have little to do with hatred of the U.S. or Western civilization in general and are sanctioned by the 4th Geneva Convention.

By equating resistance against Israeli occupation with hatred for the West and terrorism, *Jihad* glosses over murder and human rights violations committed and facilitated by the Israeli army and militant settlers in the Occupied Territories and South Lebanon, and blames the victims of Israeli aggression for their resistance. Not surprisingly, Emerson interviews an informant who accuses Rabbi Meir Kahane's assassin of "raw, red, and violent hatred," without mentioning a single time the racist ideology and actions of Kahane and his followers.

One of the most hypocritical features of the film are *numerous disclaimers* that "the overwhelming majority of Muslims are not members of militant groups", and that "Islam as a religion does not condone violence." Such statements are merely vehicles for the producer to show that he adheres to the discourse of political correctness. While the documentary's sole aim is to "prove" that there exists an Islamic fundamentalist network in the United States, Emerson leaves an escape route to distance himself from accusations that he produced an anti-Muslim film.

Many observers and analysts believe that Emerson attempts to draw a distinction between "good" Muslims and "bad" Muslims, while creating his own definitions of both. A "good" Muslim, according to Emerson's view, would not be politically active, would not be opposed to the Israeli occupation of Palestine, and would not be a member of any Muslim organization, particularly the mainstream ones, since, according to Emerson, they have all been co-opted by radical extremists.

A "bad" Muslim, according to Emerson statements, is likely to be Arab, Palestinian, politically active, and against the continued Israeli occupation of Palestine, the peace process, and American foreign aid to Israel. "Bad" Muslims also give to Muslim charities, especially those who serve the Palestinians in Palestine. They join Muslim organizations and see Islam as an international brotherhood, rather than a nationalistic religious expression. "Extremists" are vocal and activist in Emerson's opinion.

Emerson's disclaimers clash with the logic of his theory of a global terrorist network. Emerson states that the "radical fundamentalists" have nothing to do with mainstream Islam, and that they "represent only themselves – an extremist and violent fringe." If this is the case, the documentary's theme of a global fundamentalist network is untenable. If fundamentalists operate in a vacuum isolated from so-called "mainstream" Islam, why is their movement tagged "Islamic."

The message of *Jihad* is diametrically opposed to Emerson's disclaimer that fundamentalist differ from "mainstream" Muslims. Emerson implies that there exists an informal support system for radical fundamentalists among American Muslims. For the sake of political correctness, the film never verbalizes this message, but instead constructs disclaimers that run counter to its message. As will be shown later, Emerson's writings are often similarly prevaricating, but particularly in provincial pro-Israeli publications he tends to reveal his true opinions.

The release of *Jihad in America* caused a storm of protest among American Muslims. A number of crimes committed against individual Muslims or Muslim organizations after it aired indicates that its message pitted common Americans against people of different cultural backgrounds who were purportedly endangering the "American way of life," although in most cases these Muslims were also Americans. In fact, more than 60 percent of the Muslim population in America are American-born Muslims, whose descendants came to America two centuries ago.

Pro-Israeli organizations such as the Heritage Foundation eagerly exploited the terrorism scare caused by *Jihad*.

An invitation to a panel discussion on "Legal Responses to *Jihad in America*" (December 13, 1994) announced that

> The recent PBS documentary, *"Jihad in America:*
> *An Investigation of Islamic Extremists' Activities in*
> *the United States,"* outlines a significant level of
> activity by extremist groups in this country.
> Indeed, as last year's Wold Trade Center attack
> underscores, the United States cannot view itself
> as immune from the threat of terrorism.

Emerson received numerous invitations to speak on pro-Israeli and terrorism panels. The pro-Israeli Washington Institute for Near East Policy (WINEP) organized a roundtable on "Terrorism Against Peace: The International Dimensions" (November 29, 1994) with Steven Emerson, former FBI official Oliver "Buck" Revell, (who was one of Emerson's main sources in *Jihad*), and Kenneth Katzman, the author of *The Warriors of Islam: Iran's Revolutionary Guards.*—B'nai B'rith invited Steven Emerson to speak to its Board of Governors on January 22, 1995.

Together with numerous intelligence officers, Emerson was invited to speak as a terrorism expert at the Tenth Annual International Conference on Criminal Justice Issues held at the University of Illinois at Chicago (July 31 - August 3, 1995).

The Aftermath of *Jihad*

The Oklahoma City bombing which was carried out by a white American in April 1995, proved the influence of *Jihad* on the media. Steven Emerson was among the most vocal spokespersons of the theory that the bombing was the work of Islamic fundamentalists, since in his opinion Oklahoma City "is probably considered one of the largest centers of Islamic radical activity outside the Middle East."[13] On April 20, 1995 he declared on CNN that

> This is not the same type of bomb that has been traditionally used by other terrorist groups in the United States other than the Islamic militant ones.[14]

The implication is that Muslims had been responsible as a group for other domestic bombings. On *Crossfire* he stated that the bombing "is not a type of activity that has been seen on American soil prior to Islamic terrorist activity period."[15] On *CBS This Morning*, he mused

> I think the presumption is that it was a terrorist act, and there is increasing information leading authorities in the direction of a Middle Eastern-oriented attack from extremists based in the United States.[16]

The irony of this statement is highlighted in an article that appeared in *Chronicles* magazine exposing some very troubling facts about the Murrah building bombing. The article says that the FBI offices were mysteriously empty that day, though it was not a holiday. It also reports that a TOW missile was being stored in the basement of the building, though the Murrah building was not a military storage facility. In fact, the high number of child and infant casualties at the Murrah bombing site might be due to the fact that whoever tipped off the FBI did not inform the daycare center staff that the building had been targeted, or that a TOW missile was being stored in the basement of a government building that housed a daycare facility.

Innumerable journalists cited Emerson's interpretation of the event, and Emerson himself appeared on numerous TV shows. The public came to believe this theory because Emerson's critics did not receive comparable airtime. According to reports by Muslim organizations, within one year, there were over 300 anti-Muslim incidents, including death threats and harassment of individual Muslims and Muslim institutions.

Emerson and Pipes also encouraged the Anti-Defamation League of B'nai B'rith to initiate a campaign of intimidation and threats against the Council for the Study of Islamic Societies, and forced it to cancel a speech by Professor Sami al-Arian of the University of South Florida on *"The Impact of the Press Campaign Against Islam on Muslims in North America"* to be held at the Council's 13th Annual Conference at Villanova University (May 4, 1996).[17]

Emerson himself did not shy away from intimidating his adversaries physically or through his legal advisors.

On June 13, 1996, he heckled a news conference organized by American Muslim organizations that he considers to be supporters of terrorist groups (the Islamic Society of North America, the American Muslim Council, the Muslim Student Association of the USA and Canada, the Council on American-Islamic Relations, the National Muslim Political Action Center, and the North American Council for Muslim Women).

Shouting hostile remarks, and instructing his TV crew to pose as PBS representatives, he harassed the participants of the conference because they protested against an article defamatory of the Prophet Muhammad published by his former employer, *U.S. New and World Report.*

This was not the first time Emerson had engaged in intimidation and threat. In 1981, Saudi scholar Mazher Hameed worked on a project on Saudi oil security at the Center for Strategic and International Studies (CSIS). In November and December, Emerson demanded that Hameed reveal the funding of his project, or else he would expose a "petro-dollar connection" at CSIS. These allegations were pure speculation, and Hameed's project had received no petro-dollar support. Nevertheless, Emerson published some articles on the alleged "petro-dollar conspiracy" in *The New Republic*, and later expanded his "findings" in *The American House of Saud.*[18]

Another case of intimidation by Emerson occurred after *Jihad in America* was aired. Shortly after journalist Robert Friedman published an article questioning Emerson's reliability and professionalism,[19] he reportedly threatened at least four Israeli embassy officials and a reporter for *Ha'aretz* with libel suits for talking to Friedman.[20]

To fully understand the motivations behind the documentary, and anticipate the future machinations of Emerson and his editorial consultant Khálid Durán, it is necessary to closely scrutinize the worldview of both individuals. Both likely will continue to market themselves as "terrorism/fundamentalism experts," attempting to sway public opinion as well as the U.S. government in favor of their views. Already, they found imitators in the Associated Press series *Jihad USA* by Richard Cole (aired in May 1997), and *Path To Paradise* (aired by HBO in June 1997).

When South Carolina state Board of Education member Henry Jordan commented "Screw the Buddhists and kill the Muslims," he explicitly referred to *Jihad in America.*

A minority but vocal group of militant Muslims are pledged to a *"Jihad"* (holy war) to overthrow us by violent means if peaceful conquest is not successful. [...] There have already been centuries of struggle between Islam and Christianity, some of which has ended in conflict. This fact also was recently pointed out in a PBS special entitled *Jihad in America*. Currently, Israel also faces the same implacable foe, which is committed to the destruction of that democratic nation.[21]

Notice that this statement portrays Islam as the common enemy of both America and Israel, and calls upon Christian "Crusaders" to continue the "centuries old" struggle against the historic enemy of democracy, "Islam." Mr. Jordan's statement shows how successful the Emerson media blitz against Muslims and Arabs has been, while demonstrating the true objectives of this campaign.

It is likely that Emerson's propaganda will continue to influence public opinion. Emerson seemingly has made it one of his life goals to hunt down conspiracies. If there are no conspiracies around, he has remarkable skills to invent them. In the 1993 edition of *Contemporary Authors*, he mentioned under the category *Work In Progress*: "Investigating conspiracy culture and American media."[22] It is reported that he is already raising funds for a new PBS documentary on the World Trade Center bombing, and is sill working on a book on "militant extremist networks," *Mohammed's Army: The Rise of Islamic Fundamentalism*,[23] which has been funded by the Olin Foundation.

STEVEN EMERSON PROFILE

A self-described loner, Emerson was born in 1954, and received his MA in Sociology from Brown University in 1977.[24] An English teaching assistant described him as "the worst writer in the class." Emerson worked as a student coordinator for presidential candidate George McGovern in 1972, and after graduation joined the staff of Democratic Senator Frank Church (ID), then chairman of the Senate Foreign Relations Committee, where he assisted with U.S. aid to Israel. In 1978, he served on the staff of Church's Senate subcommittee investigating Aramco and Saudi oil production.

Work on the committee opened many doors to this left-leaning activist. His first target was Saudi Arabia. Alarmed by the sale of AWACS planes to the Saudi kingdom in 1981, he wrote an article on an alleged "petro-dollar connection" for the *New Republic*,[25] and wrote his first book, *The American House of Saud: The Secret Petrodollar Connection*,[26] in which he intended to dismantle the "popular perception ... that the Arab lobby pales in significance when compared to the strength and effectiveness of its counterpart, the Israeli lobby - or the Jewish lobby."[27]

In analogy to traditional anti-Semites who argue that rich Jews use their money to buy political influence, he developed the hypothesis that the petro-dollar rich Arab lobby manipulated naïve and uninformed politicians without any check from other organizations. Reviewers have pointed out that most chapters in *The American House of Saud* are seriously flawed, and that Emerson possesses an "astonishing ability to identify people falsely and to get his facts wrong."[28] Nevertheless, Emerson continues to investigate "secret" activities that he considers potentially dangerous to Israel. At the same time he has developed close ties to conservative and neoconservative Israeli circles. His associate Khálid Durán confirmed that "he has close ties to Israel,"[29] and according to investigative reporter Robert Friedman, high-ranking Likud officials such as Yigal Carmon, and Yoram Ettinger "stay in Emerson's apartment on their frequent visits to Washington."[30] Emerson never denied these charges.[31]

Between 1985 and 1989, Emerson worked as an investigative reporter for *U.S. News and World Report*. Interested in political extremism since his MA thesis on the roots of German National Socialism, he chose to specialize in the Middle East. "My specialty is to go into areas others won't touch because they're too dangerous or too much work."[32] A fascination with totalitarian regimes, secret movements and conspiracies remains one of the trademarks of all his articles and books.[33]

Since his work for *U.S. News*, Emerson has made himself an "expert" on various aspects of the Middle East, and politics related to covert actions. He has produced articles on Middle East terrorism, the security of U.S. embassies abroad,[34] U.S. anti-terrorism measures, Communist espionage,[35] the possible return of the communist threat,[36] the Iran-Contra affair,[37] and the Pan-Am bombing.[38] However, until the early 1990s, he remained a minor figure in the field of international terrorism. Herman and O'Sullivan do not even mention him in their 1989 pantheon of "terrorism experts."[39] The situation changed after he left *U.S. News* in 1989 and worked as a freelance journalist for CNN. Since that time, he frequently published contributions on Middle Eastern terrorism in the *New York Times*, and the *Wall Street Journal*. In the early 1990s, he became involved in covering the Palestinian *intifadah*, blaming the press for what he calls its "pro-Palestinian bias." One of his favorite themes are crimes committed by Palestinians against other Palestinians.

Emerson has single-mindedly pursued a media campaign comprising two main features, which he continues to repeat almost *verbatim* in each and every one of his "stories."

First, he intends to convince the public and policy makers that radical Islamic fundamentalists have infiltrated the United

States. But his articles never make it quite clear if these funda-mentalists are driven by their own anti-Western ideology, or if they are supported by "terrorist states" such as Libya, Iran, Syria. The only thing that is clear for him is that the fundamentalists are driven by their "deep hatred for Western civilization."

His second goal might be to prevent a pro-Arab or Muslim view from becoming an influential voice in political discourse in the United States. He continues to point out that Israel – which in his view is a member of Western civilization – is under siege by fundamentalists operating in the United States and in the Middle East. In his opinion, Israel requires the same pro-tection against terrorism as the United States, because Israel "alone will not be able to shut down the worldwide network of radical Islamic terror."[40] This statement further links the United States to Israel's anti-terror wars by implying that Israel and the United States are allies against a common Islamic and Arab foe.

EMERSON'S WORLDVIEW

Fake Humanism and Concern for "Mainstream Islam"

In the documentary *Jihad in America* Emerson postures himself as a humanist expressing his sincere concern for the welfare of "mainstream Islam" and the Palestinian people. However, under close scrutiny, it becomes clear that these statements are tailored for the critical audience of major newspapers like the *Washington Post*, and the *New York Times*. The same is true for his testimonies in Congressional Hearings. When he writes for neo-conservative and pro-Israeli journals, or for the commen-tary section of the *Wall Street Journal*, his "humanitarianism" vanishes.

Sound bites deliberately planted to mislead his audience abound in Emerson's writings:

Terrorism has nothing to do with mainstream Islam. Islam is an incredibly rich and peaceful religion that has given the world a wonderful legacy.[41]
The overwhelming majority of the more than seven million Muslims in the U.S. are of course law-abiding people who do not condone terror.[42]
Islam is the fastest growing religion in the U.S., and the vast majority of Muslims in America are peaceful and law-abiding and do not condone violence.[43]

There is a distinct pattern to the way Emerson uses such phrases. He usually starts with the apocalyptic scenario that the United States has become a major haven for radical fundamentalists, whose ideology is detrimental to Western culture. Immediately afterwards, he emphasizes the numerical strength of Islam in the United States. In connection with the introductory paragraphs, this is more than just a statement of facts. It could imply that there is a large pool of potential terrorists in America.

He then inserts his disclaimers. After the disclaimer, Emerson "analyzes" in detail the elaborate fundamentalist network in the United States. Frequently, he wraps up an article (like in *Jihad*) with another disclaimer, cautioning that "mainstream Muslims" might be lured into the fundamentalist network. The sequence of these disclaimers tends to vary depending on the nature of the article.

A section from an article in the *New Republic* deserves full quotation, since it vividly elucidates this strategy. Emerson writes:

With the American Muslim population of 5 to 6 million, radical groups and their adherents represent only an extremist fringe. Their militant interpretation of Islam does not reflect mainstream Islam, which eschews violence and thoroughly repudiates terrorism. But Muslim organizations are increasingly succumbing to the influence of militant Islam. "Islamic fundamentalists now control many of the Muslim organizations in the United States," says journalist Ahmed Said Nasr. As a result, Nasr says, "There is more genuine intellectual freedom of expression for Muslims living in Cairo than in the United States."[44]

Besides paying lip service to political correctness, references to mainstream Islam also fulfill the function of cautioning the reader that the moderates, too, might become fundamentalists one day. The implied message, therefore, is that moderate Muslims cannot be trusted because they are potential fundamentalists.

In pro-Israeli and neo-conservative publications, Emerson reveals his true attitude toward Islam. In such publications, he does not bother to distinguish between Islam and Islamic fundamentalism as he does in the major news media. In *The Jewish Monthly* he states:

The level of vitriol against Jews and Christianity within contemporary Islam, unfortunately, is something that we are not totally cognizant of [...]. We don't want to accept it because to do so would be to acknowledge that [Islam] sanctions genocide, planned genocide, as part of its religious doctrine. [...] Unfortunately, nearly all of the Islamic organizations in the United States that define themselves as religiously or culturally Muslim in

character have, today, been totally captured or
dominated by radical fundamentalist elements.[45]

In the *San Diego Union Tribune*, he analyzes the World Trade
Center bombing and concludes:

> There are important lessons for the future.
> Islam. The sooner Americans realize that no
> compromise or reconciliation is possible, the
> sooner radical fundamentalism will realize that
> the West cannot be manipulated.[46]

In the original article published in the *Wall Street Journal*,
Emerson qualified his evaluation of Islam, and referred only to
radical fundamentalists.

> There are important lessons for the future. First,
> radical Islamic fundamentalism cannot be rec-
> onciled with the West. The hatred of the West by
> militant Islamic fundamentalists is not tied to
> any particular act or event. Rather, fundamen-
> talists equate the mere existence of the West—its
> economic, political and cultural system—as an
> intrinsic attack on Islam. The sooner Americans
> realize that no compromise or reconciliation is
> possible, the sooner radical fundamentalists will
> realize that the West cannot be manipulated.[47]

In the *Arizona Republic*, he stresses the basic incompatibili-
ty between Western civilization and Muslim fundamentalists,
and suggests tough actions against those who do not accept the
premises of Western civilization. "Unless we ultimately get a
handle on how to stop illegal immigration or to deport people
once they are here, the problem is going to get worse."[48] This

follows in the spirit of the anti-terrorism legislation, but in Congressional Hearings and op-ed pieces to the major newspapers, Emerson never verbalizes his goal quite as drastically as he does in the southwestern border state of Arizona.

Finally, Emerson accuses all those who fail to agree with his interpretation of fundamentalism as anti-American and an accomplice of terrorism.

In the *New York Post*, Emerson blames "the politically correct atmosphere that has enveloped this country" for the fact that many U.S. policy makers "refuse to condemn Islamic fundamentalism" that "is resolutely incompatible with the West." In the same article, Emerson labels all those who oppose his interpretation of fundamentalism "apologists ... who obsessively hate Israel and the U.S." Such a statement is tantamount to accusing divergent opinions of treason. Dogmatic nativism coupled with uncritical support for Israel are thus the hallmarks of Emerson's worldview.

According to his audience, he modifies his message. For conservative, pro-Israeli, and provincial publications he postures as an anti-Islamic nativist determined to defend the purity of American civilization. For a more worldly audience he pretends to be a humanist whose sole goal is to prevent violence against innocent civilians, be they Christians, Jews, or "mainstream" Muslims.

This is a Big Country, Someone's Got to Terrorize It:[49] *The Global Network of Islamic Fundamentalist Conspiracies*

> To report leads as facts, without confirmation is not journalism. ...to get around their lack of evidence, they [journalists] pin their conspiracies on 'super sources': Often con artists and charlatans who claim to have insider knowledge.[50]

No one could have summarized his own work more appropriately than Emerson himself. To excuse him for his possible ignorance or naïveté would ignore that he is engaged in a deliberate campaign to muster support for pro-Zionist groups under the pretense of defending Western civilization. His alleged fundamentalist conspiracy consists of five elements, which he ceaselessly repeats almost verbatim in various publications and Congressional hearings:

They Hate Western Civilization in general and the United States in Particular

In Emerson's view, fundamentalists hate the West, and he repeats this message *ad nauseam*. In this view, general hatred toward other religions, and a misinterpretation of historical enmity between West and East account for this attitude. In the *Wall Street Journal*, he declared:

> The undeniable fact is that the agenda of such terrorist groups cannot be reconciled with Western notions of what constitute 'legitimate grievances'. Their hatred of Jews, Christians, secularists, and the West in general is unrelenting. To these radical groups, 'peace' is nothing more than the continuation of the Zionist-infidel conspiracy waged against Islam since the Crusades. Nothing will satisfy them until the infidels have been defeated.[51]

In testimony before Congress he stated:

> Radical Islamic fundamentalists see the West as a threat to Islam and a part of an ongoing international conspiracy stretching back to the times of the Crusades to subjugate Islam."[52]

In another Congressional Hearing he said:

> Radical Islamic militants see the very existence
> of pro-Western nations, such as Israel and
> Egypt, or pluralistic systems such as democracy,
> or rival religions such as Judaism and
> Christianity and even moderate Muslims as a
> mortal threat to their very being. These militants
> see the continuation of a thousand-year conspir-
> acy waged by the infidel to subjugate Islam.[53]

Another reason for fundamentalists' hatred is their alleged
inability to appreciate Western values and the separation of
church and state.

> Their views express an unmitigated rejection of
> the West and its systems of secularism, plural-
> ism, democracy and the separation of church
> and state, as well as unremitting hatred of Jews,
> Christians and moderate Muslims or anything
> or anything that is perceived to be a surrogate of
> the West.[54]

But what is the reason for this hatred? Emerson never provides any explanation. In his articles, irrational hatred appears
to be an innate characteristic of the fundamentalists. One cannot help getting the impression that in his view fundamentalists, even if they wanted to, would be unable to cease terroriz-
ing the West.[55]

Incapable of adhering to Western norms of interaction, "the
irreconcilable anger of militant fundamentalists ... is not sub-
ject to compromise or rational dialogue."[56] To put it differently,
Emerson seems to believe that fundamentalists reject the West
because of their hatred for Western values; – a meaningless

tautology devoid of any explanatory value, reminiscent only of the classical Orientalist technique of attributing to Islam an "essence" that accounts for every action of Muslims. In the *Arizona Republic*, he writes:

> The only definite details known about the backgrounds of the suspects [in the World Trade Center bombing] are that they were united by a zealous Islamic fundamentalist ideology: a bitter hatred of the West and its perceived surrogates, such as Western-allied Arab regimes and Israel. Under the ideology of militant Islamic fundamentalists, not only is the West's separation of church and state blasphemous, but the West, by its very existence, is deemed hostile.[57]

In the *Wall Street Journal*, he declares:

> Thus far, the only factor definitively known to link the suspects is a zealous Islamic ideology—a bitter hatred of the West and its perceived surrogates such as Western-allied Arab regimes and Israel.[58]

It is amazing that someone who majored in sociology from a top-ranking university promotes such a reductionist world view. Never is there any hint that Western colonialism, imperialism, and neo-imperialism might have something to do with counteractions in the developing world; or that some of Middle Eastern fears of Western conspiracies are justified considering the historical record of clandestine and subversive activities by Europe and the United States in the area.

There is a Fundamentalist Internationale

In order to give credence to his hypothesis that fundamentalist hatred for the West poses a real danger, Emerson develops the supporting hypothesis of a global network comprising like-minded fundamentalist organizations, whose unifying feature is their rejection of the West.

> The emergence of fundamentalist terrorist attacks in the West is part of the decentralized structure in which fundamentalists scattered around the world assume the obligation to strike blows against the West in their own communities. ... All militant radical fundamentalists are potential members of this loose federation of terrorists.[59]
>
> Radical Islamist groups are not a monolith nor are they controlled by an Islamic Politbureau. Many of the groups act independently of one another, yet often collaborate in various operations as a means of carrying out attacks on their common enemies. If there is one unifying factor among the myriad groups, it is the common enemy they confront.[60]

What makes this kind of terrorism particularly pernicious in Emerson's view is the absence of a hierarchical structure that allegedly existed when the Soviets controlled international terrorism. The result is "a new style of freelance, religion-inspired terrorism, one far harder to control than the traditional pyramidal organization of terrorist groups."[61] Besides their hatred for the West, "the myriad Islamic fundamentalist movements share a basic common agenda in promoting the resurrection of doctrinal early 7th and 8th century Islam."[62]

Apart from anecdotal references to "fundamentalist" conferences, Emerson has difficulty providing evidence for such a global terror network. He has to admit that even law enforcement agencies in various countries have so far been unable to prove the existence of such a network.[63] This does not prevent him from declaring that "even though there is no evidence that these myriad Islamist groups are centrally coordinated, it does appear that they collaborate and cross-fertilize."[64]

For lack of evidence, he only concedes the possibility of a fundamentalist network ("it does appear"). But elsewhere he pretends that he knows its existence as a fact, making an unverified hypothesis the centerpiece in his campaign. In a hearing before the U.S. House of Representatives, he omits the condition used elsewhere and states as a fact that

> These radical extremists have been able to set up a vast international network of supporters throughout the world, especially in the West, where they have amassed money and weapons, established recruitment centers, and even established command and control facilities.[65]

A mere possibility is thus elevated to a fact.

Emerson prides himself in having conducted hundreds of interviews, and sifted through "more than 150,000 documents, publications and recordings produced by radical Islamist groups."[66] What does he think this proves? Since he never deemed it necessary to learn Arabic, he has no first-hand knowledge of a large number of documents published by the groups he labels fundamentalist. It is the nature of translation that many nuances and subtleties get lost in the process of rendering one language into another. Moreover, quantity alone is no guarantee for solid investigation. It can be more insightful to analyze a small number sources correctly than to misinterpret 150,000 documents.[67] To repeat Emerson's own words quoted above: "To report leads as facts without confirmation is not journalism."

The case should also be made here that cooperation between international organizations for political, humanitarian, and religious reasons is not illegal. The Zionist international network is very vast, and meets the very description and characterizations that Emerson pins on the so-called "Islamic terrorist network."

Some "Rogue States" Sponsor the Fundamentalists

It is never completely clear from Emerson's writings what he fears most, the global fundamentalist network, or state sponsorship of fundamentalist groups. In June 1993, he argued that before the World Trade Center bombing, around 80 percent of all international terrorist attacks were state-sponsored, but that since that event there has been a shift toward "freelance terrorism."[68] However, in August 1994, he testified before the Committee on Foreign Affairs that "Iran often collaborates and networks with other radical Islamic groups", especially Hamas, and Islamic Jihad; that "Syria uses Hizbullah to attack Israeli targets in the south as an appendage of its foreign policy;" and that "Lebanon is the largest geographical terrorist base in the world."[69] The *Jerusalem Post* reprinted sections of this testimony verbatim.[70] From these contradictory perceptions of threat one again gets the impression that Emerson adjusts his statements to what his audience wants to hear.

They Are Preparing for World Rule

Following the theory of a global fundamentalist network, Emerson asserts that the war with fundamentalism will become the new battlefront of the future. "What we are witnessing is a true life drama being played out throughout the world with life and death consequences for entire nations."[71] He believes that today there exists in the United States, a vast interlocking network of activists and believers collaborating with one another from country to country. The nexus of Islamic fundamentalists stretches from Cairo to Brooklyn, from Khartoum to Brooklyn and from Gaza to Washington.[72]

The fundamentalists exploit the lenient immigration policy and the democratic freedoms of the United States, "the freest [country] in the world,"[73] to infiltrate the country, and they have "established elaborate political, financial and, in some cases, operational infrastructures."[74]

I can tell you that there are places in the United States very unsuspecting-looking hideouts or safe houses such as bakeries or gas stations or little mom and pop grocery stores, but, in fact, they're used as command centers where they actually issue instructions by fax or by telephone to carry out specific terror operations.[75]

Clustered around the religious establishment, "they use their mosques and their religious leaders to form the nucleus of their terrorist infrastructure,"[76] to recruit and instruct members in the "escalating world wide battle between radical Islamic militants and the West."[77]

Before usurping world rule, the fundamentalists will turn the United States into an Islamic theocracy. "Ultimately [their goal is] to turn the United States into an Islamic country."[78] To achieve this aim, the United States "will increasingly serve as a lightning rod for international terrorists, who perceive the United States as an enemy that must be destroyed because of its inherent evil nature."[79] In Emerson's view, the fundamentalist takeover of the United States is near: With today's infrastructure, they would be able to perform twenty simultaneous World Trade Center bombings.[80]

Another avenue toward world rule goes through Palestine. Emerson believes that Hamas's primary interest lies not in the liberation of territory occupied by Israel, but in the establishment of an Islamic empire. According to Emerson

> Hamas is a world-wide movement that feeds off the conflict in Palestine in an effort to demonstrate that the first step toward establishing an Islamic empire is through the liberation of Palestine. Hamas itself, like the other militant Islamic groups such as HizbaTahrir, Gama Islamiya and the Algerian FIS, are children of the larger pan Islamic movement known as the Moslem Brotherhood.[81]

Only the complete neglect of local conditions that dominate the actions of each of these groups allows for the formulation of a theory like this one. With such an elaborate infrastructure, why have the fundamentalists refrained from an all out attack on the United States? Emerson has the answer: "What's stopping them is the self-restraint they impose on themselves. If they commit an act of terrorism it would bring too much heat from the law-enforcement community."[82] If this is true, there is no threat.

No matter how hard one is trying to make sense of this scenario, Emerson's allegations do not add up. If law enforcement agencies intimidate the fundamentalists now, why can they not do so in the future? The impression one gets from this theory is one of the United States as a country under siege, ready to collapse by the very rhetoric of Muslim fundamentalists. It would be interesting to know how Emerson believes the Muslim takeover will happen. Through "establishing moral leadership and proselytizing individuals"?[83] Through statements of intent? Recently, he even speculates about "collaboration between neo-Nazi skinheads and some of the radical Islamic groups."[84] One wonders what comes next, a fundamentalist-KKK alliance?? Even the most conservative policy makers would discard such theories as mere paranoia. It is not surprising that U.S. foreign policy makers have a much more differentiated view of Islamic movements.[85]

They Enjoy Wide Support Among "Mainstream" Muslims, Liberal Journalists, Academicians and Democrats

Despite his disclaimers that fundamentalism has nothing to do with "mainstream" Islam, Emerson accuses the Muslim community in the United States of collaboration with the radicals, asserting that "the large local support network needed to carry out such terrorism could only arise because of the widespread acceptance of radical anti-western precepts."[86] In his opinion, a number of Muslim-American, and Arab-American organizations give legitimacy to the fundamentalists by co-sponsoring conferences, and disseminating their publications.[87] In addition, he accuses the Clinton administration of engaging in a dialogue with some of these organizations.[88] Emerson's corroborating evidence consists mainly of anti-Western statements made in Arabic publications, all of which are entirely legal, and mostly inaccessible to a large number of the Muslim-American and Arab-American community, whose native language is English not Arabic.

Repeatedly he cautions that "[t]his extremist environment, which fails to get appropriate media attention, is rapidly growing."[89] Repeatedly he blames liberal journalists, the media (such as *National Public Radio*, the *New York Times* and the *Washington Post*) and academics (such as Entelis, Esposito, Haddad and Voll) of supporting the terrorist cause. But he forgets that the media carried his documentary *Jihad in America*, and that the

New York Times and the *Washington Post* have printed a number of his commentaries and stories. Moreover, Emerson lacks both the academic credentials and the knowledge to criticize the work of internationally respected academics. In fact he never engages in any meaningful discussion of their work, except of blaming them that they are pro-fundamentalist.

The truth is that Emerson has only a minimal and often faulty understanding of Islamic history. In a testimony before the House International Relations Committee, he intended to impress his audience with references to Islamic history, but merely presented a list of outdated interpretations long discredited by serious scholars.[90] To mention some examples, he misinformed Members of Congress that

> Militant Islamic fundamentalists seek to impose
> doctrinal early 7th and 8th century Islam [...] to
> contemporary life.

This statement neglects the fact that fundamentalists are firmly rooted in Western discourse, often received their training in Western countries, and in most cases have no problem adopting modern science and technology.

In his opinion, the absence of a religious 'reformation' in Islam to a large extent accounts for the rise of fundamentalism.

This argument follows the old Orientalist thesis that the rigidity of Islam as a religion prevents development, while the Reformation infused a new dynamism into Christianity. This thesis neglects that with or without a reformation, Islam is divided into as many sects and groupings as Christianity, and it is by no way an established fact that the reformation was responsible for the development and industrialization of the West. It further neglects that the Western experience is not replicable because colonialism and imperialism have retarded the development of the non-Western world.

Modern democracies are unwilling to engage in the type of conflict that characterized religious war of previous ages.

While it is correct that democracies tend to fight fewer wars among each other, they are as aggressive against non-democracies as non-democracies are against each other. It is not clear how in the past religious wars would have been different from non-religious wars.

Christianity and Judaism, in their history, have undergone reformation, separating church from state and giving up the use of violence in the name of God.

It is hardly necessary to enumerate the wars fought by the West after the Reformation with or without reference to God. And why is violence and war in the name of secularism less objectionable than violence in the name of God?

In militant Islam, there is no separation between mosque and state, [...] between religion and politics.

Again, this reflects the Orientalist view that Islam combines religion and politics and therefore is detrimental to development. It posits a unitary Islam, ignoring differences within Islam, which have led to different regional manifestations of statesmanship. Modern scholarship has shown that in spite of the rhetoric of some Islamic scholars, in practice religion and state were almost always separate.

> During the past 16 years, radical Islamic fundamentalist movements have proliferated beyond the local regions and cities where they have been simmering since the 1940s.

How do movements "simmer"? Aphorisms like these obfuscate more than they explain. Moreover, the pan-Islamist movement reaches back to the late 19th century, and originated as an anti-colonial, anti-imperialist movement against the Western domination of the Ottoman Empire, French colonialism in North Africa, and the British occupation of India. Conflicts between Muslims, Christians and Jews arose only after the Western powers active in the Empire systematically privileged their non-Muslim clients. Under Ottoman rule, Muslims, Christians and Jews had lived together without the outbreak of large-scale violence for more than a millennium.

> Islamists articulated their rage at the West
> before the Jewish state was established.

Muslims did not oppose the West as such, but rejected colonialism and imperialism. It is therefore not surprising that the implantation of Israel onto land previously inhabited by Palestinians (Muslims and Christians) was reminiscent of the previous era of colonialism and the Mandate. Moreover, some of the most radical Palestinian groups have traditionally been secular. The rejection of Israel is a continuation of the Arabs' struggle against colonialism and imperialism during the Ottoman era and the Anglo-French Mandate, and has nothing to do with their general hatred of the Christian West.

Finally, the audience is left in the dark whether American Muslims, the media, and academics intentionally support fundamentalism,[91] or are fooled by their sophisticated strategy. Emerson laments that a "political correctness enforced by American Muslim groups has limited the public's knowledge about the spread of radical Islam in the U.S."[92] Does he imply that American Muslims are *enforcing* political correctness in order to cover the activities of the fundamentalists, or that they are the *victims* of the general climate of political correctness that Emerson disdains as passionately as do his colleagues of the New Right? Sometimes, he implies that the fundamentalists have successfully deceived "mainstream" Muslim groups into believing that there is something like moderate fundamentalism. The ambiguity as to whether American Muslims, journalists and academics are either co-conspirators with or victims of fundamentalism calls into question the validity of Emerson's theory.

Israel and the Palestinians

In Emerson's view, Israel can do no wrong, while the Palestinians have only themselves and their leaders to blame for their current predicament. Since Steven Emerson is Jewish, this opinion does not appear that controversial. Yet he never alludes to his background, and neither do others. This is possibly to prevent anyone from questioning his objectivity. "The real tragedy is that the Palestinians deserve better than Mr. Arafat. They have suffered long enough under Israeli occupation."[93] However, Emerson never looks into the effects of Israeli occupation on the Palestinian people. Would he do so, he would discover some of the reasons for the rise of fundamentalist movements. Instead, he bemoans the fact that journalists are biased against Israel, and uncritically favor the Palestinians.[94]

While one might criticize certain policies of the Palestinian Authority, Emerson presents it as a veritable demon. He indulges in accusing Arafat for sanctioning terrorism against Israel,[95] and writes extensively on murders committed by rival Palestinian factions.[96] This is certainly a topic worth investigating, but Emerson uses it to downplay the severity of the Israeli occupation. In his view, Palestine is the polar opposite of Israel. Emerson observes that after the Rabin assassination, Israeli society engaged in "critical self-analysis", demonstrating Israel's "desire for peace and affirmation of its democracy."[97] Such a generalization is meaningless, since it neglects the ongoing factional strife within Israeli society about the peace process, radical settlers, etc.

Emerson's aim is to demonstrate that Palestinians are diametrically opposed to the "democratic" Israelis: "[T]here has been no comparable recognition among most Palestinians –

nor among American Muslim and Arab organizations – that evil extremist elements exist in their own society." How can there be a "comparable" recognition in two states whose relations is determined by an overbearing asymmetry of power? Palestinians and other Arabs at length discuss issues of democracy, political culture, etc. in the Arabic-language media that are inaccessible to Emerson.

PART III

CONCLUSION

THE LONG-TERM IMPACT OF *JIHAD IN AMERICA*

Emerson and imitators of his apocalyptic message continue to enjoy a high profile in the media and in Congress. They are convinced that the U.S. strikes against the Sudan and Osama bin Laden in Afghanistan (August 1998) validated their discovery of a global Islamic fundamentalist network directed by Muslim organizations in the United States.[1]

The Anti-Terrorism Legislation

The anti-terrorism legislation in the wake of the World Trade Center bombing — whose death toll was a fraction of that in Oklahoma City — is only the most blatant example of the impact *Jihad* had on public opinion. On June 19, 1995 only a few weeks before the anti-terrorism debate, representatives Bill McCollum (R-FL) and Gary L. Ackerman (D-NY), the chairman of the House Judiciary Committee, circulated a videotape of *Jihad* to each of the 435 House members. According to Emerson, the Carthage Foundation paid for the videotapes.[2]

There can be little doubt that the documentary and Emerson's ceaseless newspaper campaign deserve credit for passing the legislation. *New York Times* commentator A.M.

81

Rosenthal summarizes the impact of Emerson's works: "Among government officials I talked to, credit for Mr. Emerson was not only acknowledged but volunteered."[3]

The Fundamentalist Christian-Jewish Coalition to Rejuvenate Conservatism: The Freedom from Religious Persecution Act

Most recently, Christian fundamentalists have been trying to exploit Emerson's crusade against Muslim fundamentalists in their attempts to demonstrate that Christianity has long suffered persecution in non-Christian societies. Their rhetoric clearly mirrors Emerson's approach. For the sake of political correctness, they publicly declare that they oppose the oppression of any religious minority anywhere in the world. This is correct only to a limited extent and applies mainly to China. Among their primary targets are Muslim countries, and their main *protégés* are Christian minorities.

Congress already reacted to this crusade against Muslim fundamentalists by passing the *Freedom from Religious Persecution Act* (May 14, 1998) and establishing a *National Commission on Terrorism* (September 17, 1998). The mastermind behind this campaign is former Reagan administration official Michael Horowitz, who ironically is a Jew, not a Christian.

On May 14, 1998, the House of Representatives passed the *Freedom from Religious Persecution Act* by a 375-41 vote. The Act threatens to ban some U.S. exports to countries that violently oppress religious minorities. It would also limit non-humanitarian aid to such countries and demand that the U.S. government oppose loans by the IMF and development banks. The Act is the pinnacle of a ceaseless campaign by Christian fundamentalists to increase their influence on Capitol Hill.[4]

Michael Horowitz kicked off the campaign for the defense of persecuted Christians with an op-ed on "New Intolerance

Between the Crescent And the Cross" in the *Wall Street Journal* on July 5, 1995. The timing of this article is significant. It is clearly a fallout of *Jihad in America*, since it was published only seven months after *Jihad* aired on PBS. The article's anti-Muslim message mirrors that of Emerson's documentary.

In his article, Horowitz deplores the growing religious intolerance in Muslim countries and singles out Egypt, Iran, the Sudan, and Pakistan as the main perpetrators of oppressing Christian minorities. He accuses the U.S. government of deliberately ignoring such practices. Never does Horowitz in his discussion of religious persecution mention the persecution of Christians in Palestine, or that Palestinians are also Christians. He never mentions that Christians are fleeing Bethlehem as a result of Jewish persecution, and in some instances are even being expelled.

> ... while Christians in Islamic countries are increasingly imperiled for their beliefs, the U.S. government has deliberately ignored their plight.

The "New Intolerance Between Crescent And Cross" thus appears as the validation of Huntington's hypothesis of the "Clash of Civilizations."

After he published his op-ed piece, Michael Horowitz became the leader of the movement. Horowitz is a former counsel to Reagan's Office of Management and Budget and a Senior Fellow at the neo-conservative Hudson Institute. Like Steven Emerson, he began his career as a liberal and decided to become a conservative closely associated with right-wing foundations and think tanks. He once wrote:

> I am Jewish, was student body president of City College of New York, taught civil rights law [at the University of] Mississippi during the sixties,

now grieve at the loss of Al Lowenstein, the
remarkable friend who most taught me to care
about the political process.[5]

Horowitz makes no secret about to whom he owes his political transformation. "The whole transformation of Conservative
philosophy was really begun by just a handful of people,"
Michael Horowitz says, and he names Richard Larry, the grant
director for the Sarah Scaife Foundation; Michael Joyce, the
grant director for the Olin Foundation; and Leslie Lenkowsky,
who once controlled grant awards for the Smith Richardson
Foundation and moved to AEI [American Enterprise Institute]
after his nomination as deputy director of the U.S. Information
Agency fell through because he became embroiled in a conflict
over the agency's blacklisting of liberal speakers.[6]

Horowitz capitalizes on his Jewish identity to muster the
support of fundamentalist Christians. He frequently presents
his cause as a universal humanitarian endeavor that tran-
scends religious affiliations. But upon close consideration it
becomes clear that in reality his strategy fits seamlessly into
the crusade against Islamism waged by Emerson, Pipes,
Huntington, and others.

Horowitz remains a Cold Warrior in search of a new
enemy. Our model is the campaign against Soviet anti-
Semitism.[7] The lesson learned during the successful campaign
against Soviet anti-Semitism is this: Whatever tyrants gain
when the world allows them to tyrannize the powerless, they
lose when the world draws a line and stops them from doing
so. The seemingly all-powerful Communists of the Soviet
Union became less formidable when they couldn't even beat
up a bunch of Jews! They then shrank from ten to two feet tall!
Arousing our determined, implacable moral conscience to protect Soviet Jews thus also caused walls around churches,
around political dissidents, to begin tumbling down.[8]

Now that state-sponsored Soviet anti-Semitism no longer exists, Horowitz finds a convenient replacement in so-called Muslim "fundamentalist" states.

The campaign is primarily directed against Muslim countries and Islam in general. Like Emerson, he uses frequent disclaimers about "moderate" Muslims. Like Duran, he follows the Orientalist paradigm and asks Muslims to join Western civilization.

> In today's battle for the soul of Islam, vulnerable Christian communities are the battlegrounds in which the struggle is waged. Protecting them protects the Muslims who now struggle, to date without support, to leave the Dark Age prisons of the modern-day Kharajites and to enter the 21st century.[9]

Horowitz further claims that he is doing "moderate" Muslims a favor with his campaign.

> In fact, efforts on behalf of persecuted Christian communities in Islamist areas of the world [sic!] are vital means of helping moderate Muslims who are also targeted by radicals seeking to capture the soul of their great, historically tolerant faith. ... If allowed to get away with persecuting Christian communities, tyrants are able to send "you're next" messages of intimidation to everyone else they seek to oppress.[10]

Finally, there is little substance to Horowitz's claim that he speaks for all persecuted religious minorities. As he made clear in his op-ed piece in the *Wall Street Journal*, he is mainly concerned with Muslim countries in the Middle East. The only exception is Communist China, a traditional adversary since the time of the Cold War. In a hearing before the Senate Foreign Relations Committee, he introduced his speech as follows:

> In helping to shatter the silence that has for so long accompanied the persecution of Christian communities in the Middle East (and elsewhere), I believe that the Committee honors the highest American traditions precisely as it also protects America's vital interests.[11] ...
> The people with at least as much at stake in the battle against Christian holocausts and persecution are the moderate Muslims who are pawns in a battle going on for the soul of Islam.[12]

In spite of his attempts to posture as a humanitarian concerned with the wellbeing of Christians, Jews, and "moderate" Muslims alike, many of the "persecuted" Christians Horowitz claims to defend have distanced themselves from his efforts and the *Freedom from Religious Persecution Act*. For example, the Egyptian Coptic Church,[13] Anglican Bishop Sammy Azariah, Moderator of the Church of Pakistan, and Rev. Canon Clement Janda, General Secretary of the All Africa Conference of Churches expressed their displeasure. Rev. Dr. Soritua Nababan, past secretary of the Communion of Churches in Indonesia cautioned:

> The good intention of the American people to make sure that everybody in the world can enjoy religious freedom, religious liberty, may, at the end, produce more suffering for the people.[14]

The National Council of Churches (NCC), international human rights organizations, and the U.S. State Department are similarly critical of Horowitz and the Act. For example, Joan Campbell, general secretary of the NCC cautions that the

Freedom from Religious Persecution Act will jeopardize long-standing and often fragile relationships between Third World Christians and their societies.[15]

NCC associate general secretary Albert Pennybacker, emphasized that sometimes the "evangelical zeal of outsiders" has provoked unpleasant behavior toward Christians. He dismissed as "excessive and exaggerated" the claim that persecution of Christians around the world is worse than that of other religious groups.[16]

Ken Roth, executive director of Human Rights Watch, opposes the idea of focusing solely on religious persecution, instead of considering religious, gender, ethnic, and other forms of persecution.[17]

Who supports the Freedom from Religious Persecution Act?

In the light of such opposition, it is not surprising that Horowitz had to struggle to find supporters for his cause. After the "Crescent and Cross" article, he sent letters to 150 mission boards but received no response. Only gradually did he manage to get conservative religious leaders and policy-makers interested.

Horowitz now has a strong following among conservative policy-makers and religious groups. A conference on "Global Persecution of Christians" on January 2, 1996, for example, assembled the leaders of about 40 evangelical and Catholic groups such as the National Association of Evangelicals (NAE) and the Southern Baptist Convention. Also present were former Nixon aide Chuck Colson and Bao Lord, wife of former U.S. ambassador to China, Winston Lord. The NAE promptly issued a "Statement of Conscience" (drafted by Horowitz), which urged the Clinton administration to take action against Christian persecution worldwide.

While the White House rejected the NAE's demands, Horowitz and his followers managed to gain favorable reviews in the media. On January 9, 1996, Stephen Rosenfeld wrote in the *Washington Post* that Horowitz's movement represented "the most intriguing early foreign policy development of 1996 in Washington." [18]

One of Horowitz' associates is Nina Shea, founder and director of the Puebla Program on Religious Freedom, a conservative Catholic human rights organization. Shea provides the intellectual ammunition for Horowitz to wage his crusade. In spite of disclaimers, it remains no secret that the main concern is Islam. In her widely circulated book *In the Lion's Den: A Shocking Account of Persecution and Martyrdom of Christians Today and How We Should Respond*,[19] she argues that militant Islam, together with Communism, is the only ideology that has consistently oppressed Christians.

Shea projects the same cultural paranoia that pervades Samuel Huntington's *Clash of Civilizations*, and urges resolute actions against Islam. She argues that if the West fails to protect its religious adherents, we will strengthen the Islamic world in its belief that the West "must be the materialist, bankrupt culture the Islamic radicals claim we are."[20]

Horowitz's strategy proved successful: On May 14, 1998, the House of Representatives passed the *Freedom from Religious Persecution Act* by a 37541 vote.

The National Commission on Terrorism

Horowitz's campaign did not stop here. On September 17, 1998, the House passed legislation that will create a *National Commission on Terrorism* (H.R. 4536). Sponsored by Rep. Frank Wolf (R-VA), who was among the driving forces of the *Freedom from Religious Persecution Act*, the bill (also called the "Wolf amendment") is an amendment to a $16 billion package to fund U.S. aid programs worldwide. The *Commission* will consist of a 15-member panel of experts to examine national counter-terrorism policies and recommend ways the U.S. government can be more efficient in protecting Americans.

The commission will give undue credibility to the fundamentalism/terrorism experts around Steven Emerson and Khálid Durán. Not surprisingly, members proposed for the commission include some of Emerson's associates:

Daniel Pipes, pro-Israeli propagandist who defines himself as a neo-conservative ideologue and intellectual. He has close ties to the Israeli settler movement.

Ed Badolato, executive director of the International Association for Counterterrorism and Security Professionals. Badolato accuses nearly all American Muslim and Arab-American organizations of supporting Middle Eastern terrorism.

Steven Pomerantz, a former FBI assistant director in charge of the Criminal Justice Information Services Division (CJIS), and former chief of the FBI Counterterrorism Section. Pomerantz has ties to representatives of Israel's intelligence and military establishment.

Fouad Ajami, known for his anti-Arab and anti-Muslim opinions.

Riad Nachef, allegedly a leader of a Lebanese group called Al-Ahbash. Nachef was indicted by a federal grand jury last year for conspiracy to commit extortion. Another count charged him with using firearms during a crime of violence.

Anti-terrorism and anti-fundamentalism may become an increasingly lucrative business in the coming decades. The problem lies with indiscriminately identifying Islam and Muslims with the actions committed by a variety of religious and secular terrorist groups for numerous reasons. If demagogues like Emerson, Pipes, or Duran, together with their right-wing Christian and Zionist associates, have it their way, all Muslims will become the scapegoats for terrorist actions committed anywhere in the world.

APPENDIX I

WHAT OTHERS SAY ABOUT STEVEN EMERSON

Florida's *Weekly Planet Newspaper* Senior Editor John Sugg quotes two unnamed Associated Press reporters who said Emerson gave them a document on terrorism supposedly from FBI files:

> One reporter thought he'd seen the material before, and in checking found a paper Emerson had supplied earlier containing his own unsupported allegations. The two documents were almost identical, except that Emerson's authorship was deleted from the one purported to be from the FBI. 'It was really his work,' one reporter says. 'He sold it to us trying to make it look like a really interesting FBI document.'
>
> (*Weekly Planet Newspaper*, May 1998)

Letter to the Editor, *Wall Street Journal*, March 27, 1996

> Mr. Emerson exceeded his usual standard for paranoid propagandizing. He still can't get over his disappointment about the Oklahoma City bombing being the work of Muslims. His most

recent offering tries to paint Clinton as a friend of Muslim terrorists. The only Muslims in Mr. Emerson's world are terrorists, so it easy to see how he would make such a connection.

The Christian Science Monitor (January 22, 1996)

Moreover, since the end of the cold war, Islam is increasingly described by a coterie of writers and policy makers as a new seedbed for anti-Western aggression, replacing communism. Some journalists have made a virtual industry out of this view. The most prolific is Steven Emerson, whose film 'Jihad in America,' shown recently on PBS, describes America as a training ground for Islamic terrorism. Muslims almost universally know and loath Mr. Emerson's work, calling it biased and distorted.

Leslie Gelb, President, Council on Foreign Relations (CFR)

Mr. Gelb called Emerson a "grand inquisitor" for trying to censor a CFR publication.
(Forward, 5/10/96)

Fairness and Accuracy in Reporting (FAIR)

It's this sort of slippery use of evidence that makes people wary of Emerson's reporting.
(*EXTRA!*, May/June 1995)

There's more than a little bigotry in Emerson's obsession with Muslim terrorists."
(*EXTRA!*, July/August 1995)

The *Washington Post* called Emerson a "pro-Israel researcher and author." (August 8, 1995)

The *Jerusalem Post* said Emerson has "close ties to Israeli intelligence." (September 17, 1994)

Professor *Jack Shaheen*, author of *The TV Arab*, commented in a commentary on *Jihad in America* in the St. Louis Post-Dispatch:

> 'Jihad' is perilous television, pandering to stereotypes that feed collective hatreds.

Investigative reporter *Robert Friedman:*

> ...Emerson says that all criticism of him is venal; he puts his critics into the same camp as the Muslim fundamentalists and extremists. There is no logical link between criticizing Emerson's biased reporting and being pro-fundamentalist. That's Emerson's conspiracy theory.
> *(The Nation,* August 28/September 4, 1995)

> He gets it wrong all the time. Emerson has no credibility left. He can't get on TV and most publications won't pick him up.
> *(Weekly Planet Newspaper,* May 1998)

> For the first forty-eight hours (after the Oklahoma City bombing), Emerson was a fixture on radio and TV, waging jihad on Islam.
> *(The Nation,* May 15, 1995)

The *New York Times Book Review* said Emerson's 1991 book *Terrorist* was

... marred by factual errors ... that betray an
unfamiliarity with the Middle East and a perva-
sive anti-Arab and anti-Palestinian bias.

(May 19, 1991)

Security expert Vincent Cannistraro called Emerson "dis-
honest" and "Joseph McCarthy-like" (*Forward*, January 26, 1996).

Word has got around on what he (Emerson) is,
that he's a paid polemicist, not a journalist.
(*Weekly Planet Newspaper*, May 1998)

Terrorism Expert Tony Cooper, during a televised panel
discussion on the Dallas PBS affiliate following the airing of
Jihad in America, called Emerson's PBS program "propaganda"
and said Emerson was a "stranger to the truth."
Journalist Jane Hunter:

There are thousands of ax-grinders in journalism, pushing tantalizing stories with few verifi-
able facts. Most collect rejection slips, but
Steven Emerson finds one respectable media
outlet after another for his work, which is sometimes nimble in its treatment of facts, often cred-
ulous of intelligence sources, and almost invariably supportive of the Israeli government.
(*EXTRA!*, October/November 1992)

Media critic and journalism instructor, Reese Erlich, in a
radio commentary on *Jihad in America*, said:

Rather than illuminating a serious issue, the documentary uses McCarthyite techniques to attack
a range of legal political and religious groups ...

94

Arthur Lowrie, Adjunct Professor of International Studies at the University of South Florida:

> Emerson's two main themes were that an 'Islamic Internationale' exists and is directing an anti-Western terror campaign and that a network of Islamic terrorist cells exists throughout the United States. He failed to provide any hard evidence for either allegation.
>
> (*Middle East Policy*, 1995)

Chip Berlet wrote in 1995 in *Covert Action Quarterly*, a journal that investigates intelligence operations:

> Emerson makes unsubstantiated allegations of widespread conspiracies in Arab-American communities and brushes aside his lack of documented evidence by implying it only proves how clever and sinister the Arab/Muslim menace really is.

The Center for National Security Studies has reported:

> Steven Emerson has asserted that the FBI is severely restricted in infiltrating known extremist groups, that it has no terrorism data base like the CIA's, and that it is powerless to stop extremist groups from masquerading as 'religious' groups. All of these claims are incorrect.

John Sugg, Editor of *The Weekly Planet Newspaper*:

> It should be noted that Jihad in America was largely funded by the Carthage Foundation and

the Lynde and Harry Bradley Foundation,
widely referred to as right-wing think tanks.
Emerson constantly attributes allegations of
widespread Muslim conspiracies to unnamed
intelligence sources. And, as has been reported
in numerous articles. ... Emerson has been dead
wrong on many of his most sensational stories.

> ("The Secret War," Friday, March 20, 1998)

Martin Merzer in the *Miami Herald*:

> ... I call (Steven) Emerson, but we don't get off
> to a great start. I mention that I wrote a brief
> newspaper story about this affair last year.
> "Oh, really?" he says instantly. "What perspec-
> tive did you take? That this is a brutal Zionist
> plot against the weak, underprivileged Arab
> minority?" ...
> ... In January 1996, during a public forum to air
> complaints about his and *The Tampa Tribune's*
> coverage, Emerson seemed to take delight in
> provoking the largely Muslim audience and
> then pointing to their angry reaction as proof of
> their instability.
>
> ("The Secret War," *Miami Herald*, March 20, 1998)

Mohammad Muqtedar Khan, Editor of American Muslim
Quarterly:

> Most policy entrepeneurs like Emerson, Pipes,
> and Miller, maintain that Islamic fundamental-
> ist are inherently violent and that terrorism is a
> logical consequence of their fanatical beliefs and
> their hatred for U.S. values and power. They

want the USA to stop treating terrorism as a crime and to consider it an act of war. Emerson would also like the Executive Order against assassinations annulled so that U.S. security forces could make "preemptive assassinations" of potential terrorists who have demonstrable capability and have indicated an intent to attack U.S. targets.

("US foreign policy and political Islam,"
Security Dialogue, December 1998)

The role Emerson played may at first seem perplexing. He presents himself as a journalist, yet he handed off whwt appeared to be a major story to rivals. A closer look at Emerson;s career suggests his priority is not so much in use as it is an unrelenting crusade against Arabs and Muslims

(*EXTRA!*, January/February 1999)

APPENDIX II

STEVEN EMERSON IN HIS OWN WORDS

On The Alleged Plot To Bomb New York City Subways

The U.S. has become occupied fundamentalist territory.

(The Jerusalem Post, August 8, 1997)

On The Downing Of TWA Flight 800

Reuters news service quotes Emerson as saying he is "confident that a bomb brought down the plane." Emerson went on to say that the crash could be a plot by "the permanent floating (Islamic) militant international."

(Reuters, July 31, 1996)

I have no doubt whatsoever, at this point, that it was a bomb that brought down TWA Flight 800 — not a missile, but a bomb..."

(CNBC, *RIVERA LIVE,* August 23, 1996)

On The Oklahoma City Bombing

This (the bombing) was done with the intent to
inflict as many casualties as possible. That is a
Middle Eastern trait.

(*CBS News*, April 19, 1995)

Oklahoma City, I can tell you, is probably considered one of the largest centers of Islamic radical activity outside the Middle East.

(*CBS News*, April 19, 1995)

On the World Trade Center Bombing

CNN has learned that investigators working
with information from an informant, have now
deemed the very first call credible. That caller
claimed that the bombing was carried out by the
'Serbian Liberation Front,' a group previously
unknown to authorities. Law Enforcement officials tell CNN that with the aid of an informant
and other information, they now suspect the
bombers may be from one of the former
Yugoslav republics.["Likely Suspects Named in
Trade Center Bombing,"

(*CNN News*,March 2, 1993)

On the "Global Terror" Network

The United States, in my opinion, will increasingly serve as a lightening rod for international
terrorists, who perceive the United States as an
enemy that must be destroyed because of its
inherent evil nature. ... From the low tech
bomb—like the World Trade Center bomb
(which cost less than $3,000) and the Oklahoma

City bombs consisting of ammonium nitrate and fuel oil—to the double barometric bombs placed aboard Pan Am 103, the challenge for terrorists will be to see who can kill and maim more and more Americans.

(Prepared Testimony of Steven Emerson, U.S. Judiciary Committee, "Terrorism in the United States: The Nature and Extent of the Threat and Possible Legislative Responses," April 27, 1995)

The president and other public officials ought to stop legitimizing self-declared "civil rights" and "mainstream" Islamic organizations that in fact operate as propaganda and political arms of Islamic fundamentalist movements.

("How to Really Fight Terrorism," *Wall Street Journal*, August 24, 1998)

In the U.S., militant Islamic movements raise tens of millions of dollars a year — much of it through tax-exempt charitable organizations — which in turn transfer the money to overseas militant Islamic groups or which directly fund militant Islamic activities in the U.S.

("How to Really Fight Terrorism," *Wall Street Journal*, August 24, 1998)

If war breaks out, American institutions in Europe and the Middle East will face terror attacks ... by ... terrorists controlled by Saddam Hussein.

(*CNN News*, January 2, 1991)

Islamic fundamentalists have been able to exploit
the near-total social breakdown in the Arab world.
(Prepared Testimony of Steven Emerson,
Subcommittee of Africa, House Interna-
tional Relations Committee, U.S.
House of Representatives,
April 6, 1995)

On Islam

The level of vitriol against Jews and
Christianity within contemporary Islam [*Note
he did not say "radical Islamic fundamentalism."*],
unfortunately, is something that we are not
totally cognizant of ...We don't want to accept
it because to do so would be to acknowledge
that (Islam) sanctions genocide, planned genocide, as part of its religious doctrine." He
added that "Unfortunately, nearly all of the
Islamic organizations in the United States that
define themselves as religiously or culturally
Muslim in character have, today, been totally
captured or dominated by radical fundamentalist elements ....
(*The Jewish Monthly*, March 1995)

Recently a prominent Shaykh from California,
Shaykh Hisham Kabbani, gave a speech at the
State Department Forum in which he unequiv-
ocally condemned Islamic terrorist groups by
name. For that transgression, he was condemned and bitterly attacked by other "mainstream" Islamic groups as an enemy of Islam,
as a "Mossad" agent, and heaven forbid, as an

ally of Steve Emerson.
(International Association of Counter
Terrorism & Security Professionals
Conference; Terrorism: Trends and
Forecasts for 1999, Federal
New Service Transcript,
January 21, 1999)

First, radical Islamic fundamentalism cannot be reconciled with the West. The hatred of the West by militant Islamic fundamentalists is not tied to any particular act or event. Rather, fundamentalists equate the mere existence of the West—its economic, political and cultural systems as an intrinsic attack on Islam. The sooner Americans realize that no compromise or reconciliation is possible, the sooner radical fundamentalists will realize that the West cannot be manipulated. ... This means saying something that is politically incorrect: That all militant radical fundamentalists are potential members of this loose federation of terrorists."
(*The San Diego Union-Tribune*, June 28, 1993)

Moreover, the traditional immunity given to religious institutions can no longer apply if the battle against Islamic fundamentalist terrorism is to be won.
(*Detroit Free Press*, June 27, 1993)

On Palestinians

The Palestinians are not interested in or capable of living in peace with the Israelis. Most

Palestinians have sheer hatred for Jews. ...
(intra-Palestinian attacks)...are indicative of the
venom and brutality of Palestinian society.
(*Newsday*, October 25, 1990)

Israel went in [Lebanon] to clean out the PLO
terrorist nest and found enough weapons to
equip a 500,000-man army.
("In Lebanon, Syria Gets Away with Murder,"
Wall Street Journal (July 27, 1993): A18)

APPENDIX III

WHO STEVEN EMERSON WORKS FOR

"EMERSON: Right now, I am freelancing. I've left U.S. News now — it's about seven months. And I am working for publications as diverse as *Penthouse Magazine* to the *Wall Street Journal* ...."
(Transcript of interview on *Booknotes* program, Air date: May 13, 1990)

WHO WORKS WITH STEVEN EMERSON

Senior Editor John Sugg of Florida's *Weekly Planet Newspaper* noted the following about sources attesting to Emerson's credentials and characterizing American Muslim groups as allies of terrorists. Sugg wrote:

> These sources are Steven Pomerantz and Oliver 'Buck' Revell. Not noted is that Pomerantz and Revell are officers of the same institute, and that both have a close association with Emerson. They are hardly independent sources. In fact, the three spend most of their time nowadays

quoting each other about what excellent terrorism experts they all are. Revell is prominent in Emerson's *Jihad in America*.

There's a fourth member of the association — Yigal Carmon. A ranking member of Israel's intelligence and military establishment, he is considered to be the right even of the current Likud government. As *The Nation* has reported (and was never disputed by Emerson), Carmon was part of the 'gang of three' that spent much time lobbying Congress to derail the Middle East peace process — and Carmon even stayed at Emerson's home on his visits to the United States.

(*The Nation*, August 28/September 4, 1995
and May 15, 1995)

Carmon is part of Revell's and Pomerantz's institute — its 'Mideast Regional Director.' ... And Emerson even shuttles Carmon around to introduce him to journalists as an 'expert' on the Middle East.

Of course, these four people spend their time (and make money) out of portraying Arabs and Muslims as terrorists ... I don't think it's too extreme to conclude that, considering the involvement of a top Israeli spook with Emerson and his friends, we have something much more sinister going on than 'journalism' and an institute studying terrorism.

John Sugg, Senior Editor, *Weekly Planet Newspaper*, Tampa Florida, October 27, 1998

On August 7, 1998, the *Tampa Tribune* slipped a stunning statement into a report about attempts to free a Palestinian academic, Mazen Al-Najjar, from a Bradenton immigration jail where he has been held for 15 months based on "secret evidence" that he has ties to terrorists.

Tribune reporter, Michael Fechter, noted that another Palestinian, Ramadan Shallah, had worked with An-Najjar at a University of South Florida think tank, World and Islam Studies Enterprise (WISE), from 1991 to 1995. Then Fechter dropped this bombshell: "Shallah now says he served as the terrorist group (Islamic Jihad's) second in command at that time." There's an urgent reason for you to care about what the Tribune is up to. ...I had always hoped that the Tribune was merely misguided by Emerson who applauds the silencing of Muslims, not because of any action they have take, but because whoever is backing Emerson does not want the Muslim voice to be heard. Now, after examining Fechter's alleged background material for his claims on Nafi and Shafi, I have to conclude that something far more sinister may be going on.

(Sugg, John, "Dissection of a Lie," *Weekly Planet*, Oct. 28, 1998)

Council on American-Islamic Relations (CAIR),

Steven Emerson helped promote a man who claimed to be defecting from Pakistan's nuclear weapons program. The man told journalists that he was a Pakistani nuclear scientist who fled the U.S. fearing a Pakistani nuclear attack on India. Both the allegations and the man's credentials were later revealed as fake. This incident increased tensions between the India/Israeli military and the Pakistani Muslim government, and could have resulted in a serious confrontation between the two nuclear powers.

(CAIR, press release, Jan. 13, 1999)

NOTES

INTRODUCTION

1   *The New American*, vol. 12, no. 16, August 5, 1996, p. 27.

2   *Ibid.*

3   Frank Newport, Balanced Budget, Economy Top Priorities for Clinton's Second Term, The Gallup organization, November, 1996.

4   Imad ad-Deen Ahmad and Ahmed Yousef, *Islam and the West: A Dialog*, UASR Publishing Group, USA, 1998, p. 195.

PART I: The neo-conservative movement and the anti-muslim and Arab campaign

1   Samuel Huntington, *The Clash of Civilizations and the Remaking of World Order*, p. 256, p. 258.

2   E.g. Pierre Hassner, "The Clash of Civilizations and the Remaking of World Order," *The National Interest*, no. 46 (Win. 1996): 69-74. – Samir Amin, "Imperialism and Culturalism Complement Each Other," *Monthly Review* 48, no. 2 (June 1996): 1-11. – Mahmood Moshipouri and Gina Petonito, "Constructing the Enemy in the Post-Cold War Era: The Flaws of the `Islamic Conspiracy' Theory," *Journal of Church and State* 37, no. 4 (Aut. 1995): 773-92. – Richard E. Rubenstein, and Jarle Crockner, "Challenging Huntington," *Foreign Policy* no. 96 (Fall 1994): 113ff. – Stephen M. Walt, "Building up New Bogeymen," *Foreign Policy*, no. 106 (Spr. 97): 177-89.

3   Cf. Arthur L. Lowrie, "The Campaign Against Islam and American Foreign Policy," *Middle East Policy* (Sep. 1995).

109

4 Rivka Yadlin, "The Dialogue of Civilizations and Its Discontent," Annual Aaron and Cecile Goldman Visiting Israeli Professorship Lecture, Apr. 15, 1997. Full text available at: http://guweb.george-town.edu/oaur/pr/1997/goldman.htm.

5 Quoted in *The Party of Fear*, p. 390. For further references on relations between U.S. Christian fundamentalists and Israel, cf. ibid., p. 484, fn. 66.

6 Eric Alterman, "Star Wars Rerun," *The Nation* 263, no. 2 (July 8, 1996): 6.

7 Peter H. Stone, "Ice-Cold Warrior," *The National Journal* (Dec. 23, 1995): 3146.

8 August 24, 1996. Available at http://www.pfaw.org/pubs/rwfound/ rwtoc.htm.

9 On the policy of the *American Spectator*, cf. Dinitia Smith, "Spectator Sport," *New York Times* (July 3, 1994): sec. 6, p. 14.

10 Cf. Charles Storch, "Money Talks: Michael Joyce and the Bradley Foundation may be the Voice of the GOP's Future – For Millions of Reasons." *Chicago Tribune* (March 4, 1993): Sec. Tempo, p. 1.

11 For the funding patters of 75 conservative foundations, cf. Stefancic and Delgado, *No Mercy*, pp. 162-65.

12 People for the American Way, *Buying a Movement,*, p. 2.

13 Eric Alterman, "The Troves of Academe: Being in Possession of One's Faculties Has New Meaning at the Olin Foundation," *The Nation* 262, no. 25 (June 24, 1996): 22-24.

14 The following numbers are from the *Foundation Grants Index*.

15 Lexington, MA, Toronto: Lexington Books, 1986.

16 Boston, Toronto: Little, Brown and Co., 1987.

17 For a brief summary of Laqueur's though, cf. Herman and Sullivan, *The Terrorism Industry*, pp. 156-61.

18 Boulder, San Francisco, Oxford: Westview, 1993.

19 Robert D. Kaplan, "The Disturbing Freshness of Gibbon's *Decline and Fall*," *The Atlantic Monthly*, no. 279, no. 3 (Mar. 97): 16-17.

20 Robert D. Kaplan, "History Moving North," *The Atlantic Monthly* 279, no. 2 (Feb. 97): 21-24; 31.

21 Boston: Houghton Mifflin Co., 1990.

22 Boulder and London: Westview, 1988.

23 New York: St. Martin's Press, 1993.

24 New York: Random House, 1996.

25 New York, Toronto, Oxford: The Free Press, Macmillan, 1993.

26 *Ibid.*, p. 174.

27 *Washington Post Book World* (Jan. 16, 1994): 14.

28 James Phillips, "The Changing Face of Middle Eastern Terrorism," *Heritage Foundation Backgrounder* #1005 (Oct. 6, 1994).

29 Herman and O'Sullivan, *The Terrorism Industry*, pp. 77-81.

30 The following paragraph is based on Herman and O'Sullivan, *The Terrorism Industry*, pp. 104-6.

31 New York: Farrar, Straus & Giroux, 1986.

32 Claire Sterling, *The Terror Network: The Secret War of International Terrorism* (New York: Holt, Rinehart and Winston, 1981).

33 For a discussion of Sterling's view, see Herman and O'Sullivan, *The Terrorism Industry*, pp. 170-73, and Herman, The Real Terror Network, pp. 49-62.

34 *The Terror Network*, p. 16.

35 *Ibid.*, pp. 37-38.

36 "Ambassador Jeane Kirkpatrick and scholar Daniel Pipes are solidly pro-Israel and rather more sympathetic to the Likud than Clinton's crowd." Jonathan S. Tobin, "Neither Party Can Be Sole Vehicle for Jewish Concerns," *Jewish Bulletin of Northern California* (1995) [http://www.jewish.com/ bk960830/comm1.htm].

37 According to Lowrie, "The Campaign Against Islam," *MEQ* "is being distributed free of charge by Israeli consulates in the United States."

38 Daniel Pipes, "Same Difference: The Struggle Against Fundamentalist Islam has Revived the Divisions of the Cold War," *National Review* 46, no. 21 (Nov. 1994): 65.

39 *Ibid.*, p. 61.

40 *Ibid.*, pp. 62-63.

41 *Ibid.*, p. 64.

42 *Ibid.*

43 *Ibid.*, p. 65.

44 One of the best new works on the topic is Joel Beinin and Joe Stork, eds. *Political Islam: Essays from Middle East Report* (Berkeley, Los Angeles: University of California Press, 1997). – For other insightful studies of fundamentalism, cf. for example the works by David Hurst, Robert Fisk, Patrick Seal, or Gilles Keppel.

45 New York: St. Martin's Press, 1996.

46 New York: Carol Publishing Group, 1990.

PART II: Steven Emerson

1 "Israeli Expulsions Condemned by U.N." *New York Times*, Dec. 20, 1992.

2 "Six Palestinians Killed by Troops," *New York Times*, Dec. 20, 1992.

3 "World Leaders Attack Israel," *The Times Saturday*, Dec.19, 1992.

4 Sima Flapan, "The Birth of Israel and the Dier Yassin Massacre of Palestinians by Jewish Soldiers," cited in *The Origin of the Palestine-Israel Conflict*, 2nd ed, Berkeley, CA., Jews for Justice in the Middle East.

5 "Middle East Peace Talks Recess Amid Rancor," *The Washington Post*, Dec. 12, 1992.

6 *The Expulsion in the Western Media*, a collection of articles and selected abstracts, UASR, 1994.

7 "Mossad Linked to WTC Bombing Suspect," *The Village Voice*, March 8, 1994.

8 CBS News, April 19, 1995

9 "Israel Holding Three U.S. Arabs in Link to Militant Group," *New York Times*, Feb. 1, 1993.

10 "A Terrorist Network in America," *The New York Times*, April 7, 1993; Steven Emerson, "Israel Says that a Prisoner's Tale Links Arabs in U.S. to Terrorism," *New York Times*, Feb. 17, 1993; Judith Miller and Yossef Bodansky, *arget America*, S.P.I. Books, New York, 1993; "Task Force on Terrorism and Unconventional Warfare, House Republican Research Committee, *The New Islamists International*, Feb 1, 1993.

See also:

"The Accidental Terrorist: Coping with the New, Freelance Breed of Anti-West Fanatic," *Wall Street Journal* (June 13, 1993): 5. Note that he does not refer to the separation of church and state.

11 Cf. *Washington Post* (Nov. 17, 1994).

12 Unless otherwise noted, quotations are Emerson's statements made in the documentary *Jihad in America*.

13 *CBS Evening News*, Apr. 19, 1995, 6:30-7:00 p.m. EST.

14 Steve Hurst, "Officials, Clues May be Pointing Middle Eastern Groups," *CNN Live Report*, Apr. 20, 1995, 7:21 p.m. ET.

15 *Crossfire*, CNN, 7:30 p.m. ET.

16 *CBS This Morning*, Apr. 20, 1995.

17 *Jewish Exponent* 199, no. 18 (May 8, 1996).

18 On the Hameed affair, cf. Paul Findley, *They Dare to Speak Out* (Westport, Conn.: Lawrence Hill & Co., 1985), pp. 203-11.

19 Robert I. Friedman, "One Man's Jihad," *The Nation* (May 15, 1995): 656-57.

20 Idem., "Journalist's Jihad," *The Nation* (1995).

21 Henry Jordan, "Religion in Schools," *Charleston Post and Courier* (May 21, 1997).

22 Donna Olendorf, ed., *Contemporary Authors*, vol. 140 (Detroit, Washington, D.C., London: Gale Research), p. 133.

23 Announced in Steven Emerson, "Farewell to the Old PLO," *Wall Street Journal* (Sep. 10, 1993): 18. — Idem., "Stop Aid and Comfort for Agents of Terror," (Aug. 5, 1996): 18.

24 For biographical information, cf. Judith Colp Rubin, "Islamic Terror Stalks America," *Jerusalem Post Magazine* (Aug. 4, 1995): 7-9

25 Edwin Rothschild, and Steven Emerson, "Born Again Cartel," *The New Republic* 191 (Nov. 5, 1984): 20-21.

26 New York: Franklin Watts, 1985.

27 *Ibid.*, p. 2

28 Nathaniel Kern, review of *The American House of Saud*, *Middle East Journal* 39, no. 4 (Autumn 1985): 849.

29 Khálid Durán, "Krieg der Filme: Islamischer Fundamentalismus und political correctness in America," [War of the Films: Islamic Fundamentalism and Political Correctness in America]

Frankfurter Allgemeine Zeitung (Jan. 6, 1995): 9.

30 Robert I. Friedman, "One Man's *Jihad*," *The Nation* (May 15, 1995): 657.

31 Cf. his rejoinder in "Journalists' Jihad," *The Nation* (1995).

32 Rubin, "Islamic Terror," pp. 7 and 9.

33 Cf. also Steven Emerson, *Secret Warriors: Inside the Covert Military Operations of the Reagan Era* (New York: G.P. Putnam's Sons, 1988). — *Idem.*, *The Fall of Pan Am 103: Inside the Lockerbie Investigation* (New York: G.P. Putnam's Sons, 1990). — *Idem.*, *Terrorist: The Inside Story of the Highest-Ranking Iraqi Terrorist Ever to Defect to the West* (Villard/Random House, 1991).

34 Steven Emerson and Charles Fenyvesi, "A Who's Who" [Shi`i terrorist organizations], *U.S. News and World Report* 102 (Feb. 9, 1987): 26-27. — *Idem.*, and Robert A. Manning, "The Sound of Spinning Wheels" [Special Operations Forces], *U.S. News and World Report* 102 (Mar. 23, 1987): 21. — *Idem.*, and Brian Duffy, "The High Tech Terrorist," [Ahmad Jibril] *New York Times Magazine* (Mar. 1, 1990): 84. — "Capture of a Terrorist," *New York Times Magazine* (Apr. 21, 1991): 30-33.

See also:

Steven Emerson, Charles Fenyvesi, and Melissa Healy, "Can U.S. Buy Embassy Safety?" *U.S. News and World Report* 100 (Apr. 14, 1986): 22-23. — "Adding up the Cost of Safety," *U.S. News and World Report* 100 (May 5, 1986): 20. — "A Little Leak That Could be Lethal," *U.S. News and World Report* 101 (Oct. 1986): 6-9.

35 Ted Gest and Steven Emerson, "Is the U.S. Protected Against Terrorists?" *U.S. News & World Report* 101, no. 1 (July 7, 1986): 20-21. — "Special Tools for Special Jobs," *U.S. News and World Report* 101 (Nov. 3, 1986): 39. — Bush's Toothless War Against Terrorism," *U.S. News and World Report* 105 (Oct. 31, 1988): 25. — "Stymied Warriors," [America's Top Secret Antiterrorist Forces] *New York Times Magazine* (Nov. 13, 1988): 68.

See also:

"America's White Elephant in Moscow," *U.S. News and World Report* 101 (Oct. 6, 1986): 18-19. — "Coming: New Steps to Thwart Spies," *U.S. News and World Report* (Nov. 94, 1986): 8. — "Getting Ready for Soviet Spies," *U.S. News and World Report* 104 (June 27, 1988): 24-25. — "Exposing the Terror Trade: Details of

Communist Regimes' Involvement in Terrorism Against the West," *American Enterprise 1* (Sep.-Oct. 1990): 64-68.

36 "Where Have all the Spies Gone?" *New York Times Magazine* (Aug. 12, 1990): 16-21. In this sensationalist report on the East German Stasi, Emerson together with German officials expresses his concern "that some, perhaps many, Stasi agents will adopt a low profile, patiently waiting, as they have been indoctrinated to do, for the time when they can once again ply their trade." (p. 21)

37 "Arms-for-Hostages Deal: Dogging the Money Trail," *U.S. News and World Report* 102 (Feb. 16, 1987): 21. — *Idem.*, and Robert A. Manning, "Ollie North's Private Network," *U.S. News and World Report* 102 (Mar. 9, 1987): 16-17. — "Israel's End of the Iran Affair," *U.S. News and World Report* 102 (Apr. 13): 20. — "Back to the Beginning in the Iran-contra Affair," *U.S. News and World Report* 102 (June 29, 1987): 20-22. — "A Secret Arms Network's Ever Expanding Cast," *U.S. News and World Report* 103 (Nov. 15, 1987): 30-31. — "George Bush's Iran-Contra Albatross," *U.S. News and World Report* 104 (Jan. 18, 1988): 23-24. — *Idem.*, and Stephen J. Hedges, "Ollie North's Troubles: The Sequel," *U.S. News and World Report* 106 (Feb. 6, 1989): 24.

38 "Taking on Terrorists," *U.S. News and World Report* 105 (Sep. 12, 1988): 26-29. — "On the Trail of Terrorists," *U.S. News and World Report* 106 (Feb. 13, 1989): 36. — *Idem.*, Brian Duffy, and Richard Z. Chesnoff, "Closing in on the Pan Am Bombers," *U.S. News and World Report* 106 (May 22, 1989): 23-24. — "To Catch a Terrorist," *Reader's Digest* 134 (Oct. 1989): 107-11.

39 Herman and O'Sullivan, *The Terrorism Industry*.

40 Steven Emerson, "Iran and Irrational Rage," *Jerusalem Post* (Sep. 11, 1994): 6.

41 Statement of Steven Emerson, Aug. 1, 1994, U.S. House of Representatives, Committee on Foreign Affairs, Subcommittee on International Security, International Organizations and Human Rights.

42 Steven Emerson, "The Snake of Terror in Our Garden," *Wall Street Journal* (Mar. 5, 1993): A8.

43 Steven Emerson, "The Other Fundamentalists: A Look Inside the Radical Islamist Network," *The New Republic* (June 12, 1995): 21.

44 Emerson, "The Other Fundamentalists," p. 30.

45 *The Jewish Monthly* (March 1995).

46 "U.S. Needs an Antiterrorism Strategy," *San Diego Union-Tribune* (June 28, 1993): B-7.

47 "The Great Satan Wins One," *Wall Street Journal* (June 25, 1993): A10.

48 Steven Emerson, "The New Face of Terrorism: World Trade Center Served as a Wake-Up Call for the West," *The Arizona Republic* (July 11, 1993): C1.

See also:

Steven Emerson, "The Threat to the West: It's Time to Face Facts — Islamic Fundamentalism is Waging an Ongoing Holy War," *New York Post* (June 28, 1993).

49 Emerson on Fox Television (Apr. 1995), quoted in Thomas Friedman, *"Journalist's Jihad," The Nation,* (1995).

50 Steven Emerson, "Ross Perot's Conspiracy Fever — And Ours," *Wall Street Journal* (Oct. 28, 1992): A18.

51 "Diplomacy That Can Stop Terror," *Wall Street Journal* (July 22, 1994): A10

52 Testimony, Subcommittee of Africa, House International Relations Committee, U.S. House of Representatives, Apr. 6, 1995.

53 Statement by Steven Emerson, U.S. House of Representatives, Committee on Foreign Affairs, Subcommittee on International Security, International Organization and Human Rights, Aug. 1, 1994.

54 Prepared Testimony, House of Representatives, Subcommittee of Africa, House International Relations Committee, Apr. 6, 1995.

55 "To these groups, there can be no compromise; it is a duel to the death with infidels and heretics." Testimony, U.S. House of Representatives, Committee on Foreign Affairs, Subcommittee on International Security, International Organizations and Human Rights, Aug. 1, 1994.

56 "Terrorism and the Middle East Peace Process: The Origins and Activities of Hamas in the United States," Testimony, U.S. Senate, Subcommittee on the Near East and South Asia, Mar. 19, 1996.

57 "The New Face of Terrorism: World Trade Center Served as a Wake-Up Call for the West," *The Arizona Republic* (July 11, 1993): C1. See the identical phraseology in "A New Terrorism: Islamic Fundamentalism's Terrible Threat to the West," *The San Diego*

Union-Tribune (June 27, 1993): G-3.

58 "The Accidental Terrorist: Coping with the New, Freelance Breed of Anti-West Fanatic," *Wall Street Journal* (June 13, 1993): 5. Note that he does not refer to the separation of church and state.

59 "The Great Satan Wins One," *Wall Street Journal* (June 25, 1993): A10.

60 Testimony, U.S. House of Representatives, Committee on Foreign Affairs, Aug. 1, 1994.

61 "The Accidental Terrorist," *Washington Post* (June 13, 1993): C5.

62 Prepared Testimony of Steven Emerson, Subcommittee of Africa, House International Relations Committee, U.S. House of Representatives, Apr. 6, 1995.

63 "The Accidental Terrorist," *Washington Post* (June 13, 1993): C5.

64 "The Other Fundamentalists: A Look Inside the Radical Islamist Network," *New Republic* (June 21, 1995): 22.

65 Testimony, U.S. House of Representatives, Committee on Foreign Affairs, Aug. 1, 1994.

66 "The Other Fundamentalists," p. 21.

67 In all fairness, it has to be emphasized that linguistic skills alone do not compensate for analytical rigor.

68 "The Accidental Terrorist," *Washington Post* (Jun 13, 1993): C5.

69 Testimony before the U.S. House of Representatives Committee on Foreign Affairs, Subcommittee on International Security, International Organizations and Human Rights, Aug. 1, 1994. — For the same line of argumentation, cf. "Diplomacy that an Stop Terror," *Wall Street Journal* (July 22, 1994): A10.

70 "Iran and Irrational Rage," *Jerusalem Post* (Sep. 11, 1994): p. 6.

71 Testimony, Subcommittee of Africa, House International Relations Committee, U.S. House of Representatives, Apr. 6, 1995.

72 Testimony, U.S. Senate Judiciary Committee, Apr. 27, 1995.

73 "Get Ready for Twenty World Trade Center Bombings," *Middle East Quarterly* 4, no. 2 (June 97): p. 75.

74 "The Other Fundamentalists," p. 21.

75 *MacNeil/Lehrer News Hour* (Oct. 20, 1994).

76 "The Great Satan Wins One," *Wall Street Journal* (June 25, 1993): A10.

77 Testimony, U.S. House of Representatives, Committee on Foreign Affairs, Subcommittee on International Security, International Organizations and Human Rights, Aug. 1, 1994.

78 "Get Ready for Twenty World Trade Center Bombings," p. 74.

79 Testimony, Senate Judiciary Committee, Apr. 27, 1995.

80 "Get Ready," p. 72.

81 "Terrorism and the Middle East Peace Process."

82 Rubin, "Islamic Terror Stalks America," p. 9.

83 "Get Ready for Twenty World Trade Center Bombings," p. 75.

84 "Extent to Which Terrorists Profit on American Soil," *The Latest on the Mary Matalin Show* (CBS Talk Radio Network), July 31, 1996, 3:00-3:30 p.m. EST.

85 For a concise summary, cf. Joel Beinin and Joe Stork, "On the Modernity, Historical Specificity, and International Context of Political Islam," in *Political Islam*, eds. idem. (Berkeley, Los Angeles: University of California Press, 1997), pp. 16-19.

86 Testimony, U.S. House of Representatives, Committee on Foreign Affairs, Subcommittee on International Security, International Organizations and Human Rights, Aug. 1, 1994.

87 "Stop Aid and Comfort for Agents of Terror," *Wall Street Journal* (Aug. 5 1996): A18.

88 "Friends of Hamas in the White House," *Wall Street Journal* (Mar. 13, 1996): A14.

89 "Get Ready," p. 75.

90 All subsequent quotations are from Prepared Testimony, House of Representatives, House International Relations Committee, Subcommittee of Africa, Apr. 6, 1995.

91 "There exists an effective alliance between some radical Islamic factions and leftist groups, including such publications as *The Village Voice and The Nation*." "Get Ready," p. 79.

92 "Stop Aid and Comfort," p. 18.

93 "Arafat's chronicle of betrayal, " *Wall Street Journal* (May 5, 1994)

94 Rubin, "Islamic Terror Stalks America," p. 8.

95 "Farewell to the Old PLO," *Wall Street Journal* (Sep. 10, 1993): A18. — "Missing Peace: Arafat's Silence About Fundamentalist Terrorism Undermines the Accord," *Washington Post* (Nov. 7, 1993): C2.

96 "Meltdown: The End of the Intifada," *The New Republic* (Nov. 23, 1992): 26-29. — "The Intifada You Don't See on TV," *Wall Street Journal* (Feb. 21, 1990). — "Setting the Terms on Mideast Talks," *Wall Street Journal* (Oct. 22, 1992): A14.

97 "What the Rabin Killing Tells Us," *Wall Street Journal* (Nov. 7, 1995):

PART III: Coclusion

1   Steven Emerson, "How to Really Fight Terrorism," *Wall Street Journal* (August 24, 1998).

2   Kenneth J. Cooper, "Two in House Attacked for Use of `Jihad' Video," *Washington Post* (June 27, 1995). — Laurie Kellman, "Arab-Americans Blast Two on Hill," *Washington Times* (June 26, 1995).

3   A.M. Rosenthal, "On My Mind: Jihad in America," *New York Times* (Feb. 3, 1995): Sec. 3, p. 19.

4   The Rev. Jay Lintner, "The Right's Holy War," *The Nation* (July 20, 1998): 6-7.

5   Gregg Easterbrook, "Ideas Move Nations: How Conservative Think Tanks Have Helped to Transform the Terms of Political Debate," *The Atlantic Monthly* (January 1986).

6   *Ibid.*

7   National Public Radio, *Weekend All Things Considered* (December 1, 1996): 8:00 p.m. ET. Host: Daniel Zwerdling.

8   Michael Horowitz, "Address delivered to the William Wilberforce Award Dinner, Washington, D.C., February 5, 1997, in *Vital Speeches* 63, no. 15 (May 15, 1997), pp. 63ff.

9   *Ibid.*

10 *Idem.*, Testimony, Subcommittee on Near Eastern and South Asian Affairs, Senate Foreign Affairs Committee, June 10, 1997.

11 *Ibid.*

12 National Public Radio, *Talk of the Nation*, October 22, 1997, 2:00

p.m ET. Host Lynn Neary.

13 *Ibid.*

14 Quoted in Lintner, "The Right's Holy War," p. 6.

15 National Public Radio, *Talk of the Nation*, October 22, 1997.

16 David Aikman, "Rescue to the Christians: Why is the White House Ignoring the Growing Persecution of Christians Worldwide?" *The American Spectator* 29, no. 7 (July 1996): 24.

17 National Public Radio, *Talk of the Nation*, October 22, 1997.

18 Stephen Rosenfeld, "Human Rights for Christians Too," *Washington Post* (February 9, 1996).

19 Nashville, TN: Broadman and Holman, 1997.

20 Cf. Tom Bethell, "Saving Faith at State: Why Won't the State Dept. Stand up for Christians?" *The American Spectator* (April 1997).